AQA GCSE

GCSE
Revision
GUIDE

Business & Communication Systems

Jonathan Sutherland
Diane Canwell

Philip Allan Updates, an imprint of Hodder Education, an Hachette UK company, Market Place, Deddington, Oxfordshire OX15 0SE

Orders

Bookpoint Ltd, 130 Milton Park, Abingdon, Oxfordshire OX14 4SB
tel: 01235 827720
fax: 01235 400454
e-mail: uk.orders@bookpoint.co.uk
Lines are open 9.00 a.m.–5.00 p.m., Monday to Saturday, with a 24-hour message answering service. You can also order through the Philip Allan Updates website: www.philipallan.co.uk

© Philip Allan Updates 2010
ISBN 978-1-4441-0775-3

First printed 2010
Impression number   5   4   3   2   1
Year   2014   2013   2012   2011   2010

Printed in Italy

Hachette UK's policy is to use papers that are natural, renewable and recyclable products and made from wood grown in sustainable forests. The logging and manufacturing processes are expected to conform to the environmental regulations of the country of origin.

P01655

Contents

Introduction

What is Business and Communication Systems?

Business and Communication Systems links the key areas of business with the practical use of ICT applications, which include word processing, spreadsheets and databases. It is one of the new-look business and economics GCSEs.

How will I be assessed?

There are three units to study. The first has a straightforward 1-hour written examination. The second unit has a computer-based exam lasting 90 minutes. The third unit is assessed by the new version of coursework, known as 'controlled assessment'. You will have a limited amount of time to prepare, research, plan and make your final presentation on a business and communications topic decided by the examination board.

How do I use this book?

All parts of the three units are covered in order in this book. Each topic provides you with all of the basic information, along with a series of questions that you can try out for yourself to test your skills and knowledge. Working through the book systematically, you can see how **Unit 9: Using ICT in business** builds on all the basic information that you will cover in **Unit 8: ICT systems in business**. Taking the knowledge and skills from Units 8 and 9, you will then be in a position to tackle **Unit 10: Investigating ICT in business**.

Make sure that you work through all of the topics and try out as many of the questions, tasks and activities as possible. Each question has a suggested mark allocation which will give you an idea of how much time to spend on it. This is deliberate because it aims to give you the maximum amount of practice to produce the level of response you will need in a limited amount of time in the examination. It is important to remember that the basic knowledge that you cover in Unit 8, coupled with the skills that you acquire in Unit 9, provides you with all the information you need to tackle Unit 10.

We have included some suggestions of how to handle the controlled assessment for Unit 10, but it will be based on what you have already covered in the other two units.

What are the features of this book?

Each of the topics follows the AQA specification, just as it appears. The topics are set out the same format, so you will quickly know where to find the information that you need. There are a number of features in each topic:

- *What the specification requires*. This is an easier-to-understand version of the amplification from the specification. In it you may find a number of key words, which are featured in the *Speak the language* feature.
- *Speak the language.* This gives you short and straightforward definitions of key terms, phrases and jargon.
- *In brief*. If you have no time to read anything else, you should read this. It tells you why this particular topic is important and gives you the basic information.
- *Revision notes*. The main information for each topic can be found here. This is usually a set of bullet points that build on the information that was included in the *In brief* feature. This is the largest section in each of the topics.
- *In a nutshell*. This acts as a summary or a conclusion to the information that has appeared so far in the topic. Again it is structured into a number of different bullet points.
- *Boost your grade*. As you will see, the book contains tips about the different levels of response that examiners are looking for in order to award you marks. The more marks you get, the better the grade you will receive. The *Boost your grade* feature takes the topic one or two stages further on. It integrates the information, puts it into its context and suggests other things you might want to mention to gain those valuable extra marks.
- *Test yourself*. This feature includes sets of questions, tasks or activities that relate to the information in the topic. In many cases there will be a short case study before the questions. Pay attention to the number of marks that are allocated to each of the questions, tasks or activities. You should be aiming in Unit 8 for a mark a minute. In Unit 9, as you have a little extra time, it is a mark per 90 seconds. The more marks available, the longer you should spend in answering and the more complex your answer needs to be.

There are other features in the book. At the end of each unit there are section tests. These are divided into relatively straightforward questions or activities and more complex ones where you need to justify, evaluate and explain your answers. All of these have case studies, which are similar to those that you will find in the examination. At the end of each unit there is also a practice exam. This follows the same format as a real exam paper, with real instructions and spread of marks.

Suggested answers to all the questions in the book are available online at **www.hodderplus.co.uk**. Here there is also a great deal more information that you might find useful, particularly when you have to apply business terms or ICT concepts and jargon to situations.

Revision tips

Obviously you need to start revising as early as possible. This might be complicated because the way this new GCSE is structured might mean that you will take your examinations at different times of the year. However, you will need to have covered all of Unit 8 before you can sit that examination. You will also need to put in as much practice work as possible on a computer, so that you are confident enough to sit the computer-based examination for Unit 9. It is also likely that the last examination that you sit will be Unit 10, because you will need to have covered the other two units first.

Because the three examinations are all different you can tackle them in different ways:

- *Unit 8*. This needs to be revised like an ordinary exam, so you need to go through all of the Unit 8 topics and make sure that you remember and understand as many of the terms and concepts as possible.
- *Unit 9*. You need to know how and why different software is used and you will also need as much hands-on practice on a computer as possible.
- *Unit 10*. If you are confident about the first two units, all you really need is good organisation and planning to tackle Unit 10. It is not that much different from coursework. The differences are that you have less time and you are supervised throughout all of the sessions and will have to hand the work back in at the end of each session.

Unit 8
ICT systems in business

What is the unit about?

Unit 8 aims to explain the importance of information and communications technology in business. It shows how ICT contributes to a successful business and also looks at different ICT systems and how they have an impact on the way in which people work. ICT is very important in improving communications. The unit also looks at potential risks, such as health and safety and the security of data.

The unit is split up into three sections:
- *Administration.* This section explains how administration supports the main functions of a business, from the moment it is set up through its growth and continued operations.
- *Human resources.* This highlights the importance of people and how they are vital in making sure that businesses achieve their objectives. It includes recruitment, retention, the rewarding of staff and providing a safe working environment.
- *Communication.* This explains the structure and importance of communication systems and how they are vital in helping businesses to meet their aims and objectives.

ICT is extremely important, as the majority of businesses use it to assist their operations and to streamline the way they work. Unit 8 provides the foundation to understand how ICT systems are used by businesses.

You will need to understand how ICT systems are used, as this will help you with the other two units, which are more practical-based. ICT has radically changed the way businesses communicate with one another and with their customers. It enables businesses to organise their work better, handle data, communicate with customers and suppliers, sell their products and services, and provide customer support.

What about the exam?

This is a conventional 1-hour written examination paper. There are 60 marks available and, in all, the exam is worth 40% of this GCSE. There are usually four sets of questions and each of them has a scenario, or item, known as 'stimulus material'. These are like short case studies. The questions relate to the case studies and may ask you about key words that have been used in the case study. Some questions will ask your opinion and you will need to explain what you mean. Other questions might be more complicated, asking you to explain a process and why it is important. The marks generally range from 1 to a maximum of around 10 per question. Each of the sets of questions after each case study is worth between about 9 and 20 marks. Pay attention to the number of marks that are available, as it gives you a clue as to how much time you should spend on each question.

How do I get a good grade?

You will probably be aware of the fact that there are three assessment objectives, AO1 to AO3. If you are answering questions for AO1 then you are just recalling or listing what you can remember. For AO2 you are beginning to apply what you know and this means applying it to the case study. For AO3 you need to analyse and evaluate; this means making a judgement and drawing conclusions about what you have said. You do not need to worry about AO3 for questions that only offer you a handful of marks; pay attention to those that are worth 7 or more marks.

Topic 1
The business environment

What the specification requires

You will need to identify the key **aims and objectives** of a business, the different **stakeholders** and how both of these considerations have a major impact on the business.

In brief

All businesses have aims and objectives; these are used to measure their success, such as gaining **market share**. Businesses also have a range of stakeholders, internal and external. Each stakeholder group has demands and expectations that the businesses must try to fulfil. This means that the business has to try to balance the often competing demands of the stakeholders. On the one hand, shareholders will want the business to maximise profits; on the other, customers will want high-quality products and services at an affordable price. At the same time, employees will want to receive a fair level of pay for their work.

The Co-operative Bank

Businesses have to balance the needs of their stakeholders

Revision notes

The most successful businesses have **mission statements** to help them meet their aims and objectives. Aims and objectives help a business to:
- make decisions
- set targets
- measure their progress
- make sure that all parts of the business are working towards the same goal

Typical aims and objectives are:
- breaking even — making sure that the income of the business is equal to its expenditure
- making a profit — ensuring that income from sales is greater than spending

- creating jobs and wealth — providing employment and building up the assets owned by the business
- survival — ensuring that the business keeps going in difficult economic times
- market share — increasing sales income compared with other businesses selling to the same market
- customer satisfaction — exceeding the expectations of customers by providing high-quality products, services and support
- being ethical — making decisions that are morally correct
- being sustainable — running the business so that it does not have a negative impact on the environment

Stakeholders influence the aims and objectives of a business and may hold different views or demand different things from the business. A business will try to rank the importance of its stakeholders and work out how powerful each of them is, then try to take each into account when it makes decisions. Pleasing all stakeholders is almost impossible. Some of the stakeholders will be internal ones, such as managers and employees; others will be external, such as customers, banks and the government.

> **Speak the language**
>
> **aims and objectives —**
> the goals of the business; aims are short term and objectives longer term
>
> **market share —** the value of a business's sales as a percentage of the total sales of all businesses operating in that market
>
> **mission statement —**
> a sentence or set of points that summarises what the business does, stands for and hopes to achieve
>
> **stakeholders —** an individual or group that is affected by a business or has an interest in the activities of a business

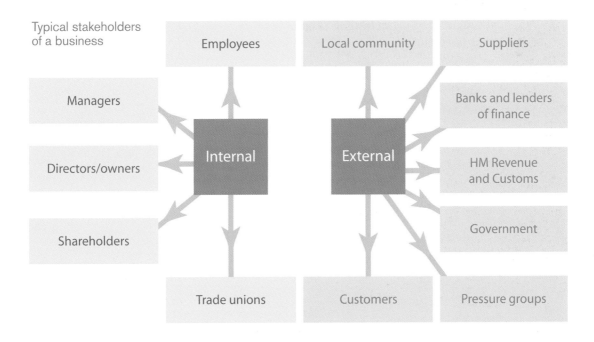

Typical stakeholders of a business

In a nutshell

Businesses create mission statements to help them understand and measure their success in meeting their aims and objectives.

* Mission statements need to be measurable.
* They need a timescale.
* They have to be clear and mean something.
* They need to be realistic.

Businesses cannot set their aims and objectives without thinking about the expectations of their stakeholders. Different stakeholders will have different demands; all will expect the business to take account of them:

* Pleasing one stakeholder group may anger another one.
* Some groups are more powerful than others.
* The bigger the business, the more stakeholder groups there are.
* The business needs to act responsibility and explain its actions.

Test yourself

Anderson's Steel Ltd has a 16% share of the £1.4 billion British market for steel fences. Its advertising slogan is 'Quality British steel products, accept no substitute' and its mission statement is 'British quality products for the world made by the experts'.

1 What is meant by 'market share'?   *(2 marks)*

2 What might Anderson's mean by their slogan and mission statement?   *(4 marks)*

3 Identify and explain the likely stakeholders of a business like Anderson's   *(9 marks)*

Boost your grade

The relationship between a major stakeholder and a business needs careful handling. The owners want the business to generate profit. However, another major stakeholder group is the business's customers and they want reasonable prices, quality products and reliable service. It is not always easy to balance the needs of these two key groups. Compromises have to be made, sometimes profits have to be cut to provide for customer needs, and sometimes customers have to pay slightly more to ensure that the business makes a profit.

Topic 2
Business administration

What the specification requires

You will need to understand that administration involves the storing, processing, retrieving and circulation of information to support the functions of a business. Each part of the organisation needs this support and information to work in an effective way. You will also need to know that there are several different job roles in any business.

In brief

Being efficient and having the ability to react to situations as they happen are vital if a business is to be successful. This means that the business has to be able to make decisions based on the latest information. It needs to circulate (disseminate) this information to all of the key departments or areas of the business. Businesses have a range of people working for them in their **hierarchy**, each with particular job titles and responsibilities.

Revision notes

Administration helps a business to coordinate its activities and allows decision makers to plan for the future. A business needs to have access to relevant information when it needs it:

- Information comes into the business.
- It is processed and passed on to relevant parts of the business.
- Copies of the information are stored.
- The information is retrieved when needed in the future.
- Decisions are made, based on the information received and processed.

PhotoDisc

Businesses need to process information efficiently

Typical administrative support is needed for:

- meetings
- creating and distributing documents
- arranging events, travel and accommodation
- handling data, documents and other information
- distributing information
- storing information in a secure manner

Administration supports the key functions of a business including:

- finance and accounts — dealing with income and expenditure, **budgets** and the creation of financial documents such as **balance sheets** and **profit and loss accounts**
- human resources — handling all matters relating to employees, including recruitment
- sales — creating orders and dealing with customers
- marketing — promoting and advertising the business's products and services
- research and development — coming up with new ideas and testing whether they work and whether customers would buy them
- customer service — handling customer queries and complaints, and providing assistance
- IT services — responsible for all the hardware and software needs of the business
- production — making the products that the business sells
- purchasing — buying all of the goods and services that the business needs
- distribution — handling the transport and delivery needs of the business

There are a number of different job roles in any business, including:

- managers — who make day-to-day decisions and organise the other employees
- supervisors or team leaders — who make sure that the day-to-day tasks are carried out
- operatives — the regular employees who carry out most of the work in the business
- support staff — who assist all of the other employees to do their job

Businesses seek to organise their workforce in the most efficient way. Most organisation charts look like a pyramid with a small number of key decision makers supported by managers, who direct the work of supervisors, who in turn organise the tasks and duties of the bulk of the employees.

Span of control

Fotolia

These layers are known as hierarchies, with each layer having certain authority and responsibility. Each manager or supervisor will be directly responsible for organising the work of a number of other employees; this is known as a 'span of control'.

In a nutshell

Administration is vital to the smooth running of a business as it means:
* All information is handled.
* It is passed on to right part of the business.
* The business has the latest information.
* It can act on this information.
* It can make the right decisions.

Each business organises itself to match its needs either by:
* what it produces — different departments for different products
* what it does — departments each have different functions
* where things are done — different departments for different areas
* whom it sells to — different departments for different customer types

Test yourself

Farman Associates has five hierarchical layers in the business. It has a dedicated department which deals with all administrative procedures. It runs a computer-based system alongside a paper-based one.

1 What does 'hierarchical layers' mean? *(4 marks)*

2 What is meant by 'administrative procedures'? *(4 marks)*

3 Why might the business have two systems? *(7 marks)*

Boost your grade Businesses need to log, circulate, store and retrieve a vast amount of information, and without a sound filing and retrieval system, crucial pieces of information can be lost or ignored.

Topic 3
Tasks, decision making and planning

What the specification requires

You will need to understand that administration has to handle **routine** and **non-routine** work, and that this may mean that managers will have to make non-routine decisions as well as regular, routine ones. You also need to remember that planning is very important in a business — without planning the business will never be prepared and organised to do anything.

In brief

Administration systems handle a great deal of routine work, but they also need to cope with non-routine work which is out of the ordinary. Day after day, routine decisions are taken by managers, but sometimes they have to make decisions about things they have not had to handle in the past. A key to being able to cope with all situations is to plan in advance; good planning is essential for continued success.

Revision notes

The activities of business, including administration and decision making, can be routine or non-routine. Some work and decisions will never differ regardless of what else is happening in the business. Other work and decisions can be different every day, but these will still need the support of good administrative procedures to ensure that the work is efficiently carried out and the right decisions are made.

Decision making involves:

- looking at the alternatives and then choosing the one that is likely to be the most successful or acceptable to all concerned
- having a back-up plan or **contingency plan** in place to help the business at a time of crisis
- meeting to get ideas and suggestions for how to solve a problem, known as **brainstorming**

> ### Speak the language
>
> **brainstorming** — a group discussion where the group looks at different ways of handling a problem and comes up with the best solution
>
> **contingency plan** — a series of actions that will be taken by the business if a crisis happens
>
> **non-routine** — activities or decisions that are unusual or only crop up from time to time
>
> **routine** — activities or decisions carried out or made on a regular basis

Planning is important for all businesses. This means deciding:

- what the objectives of the plan are
- who needs to do what to make it happen
- what needs to be done to meet the objectives
- how the business will know if the plan is working or not

The saying 'failing to plan is planning to fail' is a good one. If a business does not make plans for the future, it will not know where it is going, how it is performing or how to deal with problems when they arise. Planning aims to:

- eliminate or reduce uncertainty
- improve efficiency
- give a better understanding of objectives
- provide a basis for monitoring and controlling the business

In a nutshell

Businesses have to carry out a number of routine and non-routine tasks every day; they also will make routine and non-routine decisions.

Handling routine work and routine decisions can be straightforward if the business has set procedures to handle them. Coping with non-routine work means that managers and employees need to be flexible in their approach to work and handle these tasks as and when they happen. Making non-routine decisions is more difficult, as the business may not have encountered these problems in the past.

This can be dealt with by having plans ready to deal with problems. If a business plans ahead and considers all the problems and situations that it might face, then it is better prepared to deal with them.

Failing to plan in advance may cause the business real problems as it has to cope with the situation it is facing and keep doing all of the regular, routine work at the same time.

Ingram

Failing to plan may cause problems for the business

There are three basic kinds of decision:
- Decisions whether — these are yes/no, either/or decisions that must be made before selecting an alternative.
- Decisions which — these involve a choice of one or more alternatives from a set of possibilities. The choice is based on how well each alternative measures up to a set of criteria.
- Contingent decisions — these are decisions that have been made but put on hold until some condition is met.

Test yourself

A regular customer of a shop returns a present bought for them 3 weeks ago. Normally, the shop has a strict 14 days returns policy. On the same day, a delivery arrives, one person has to check the delivery, another has to price up the products and another has to contact the supplier as part of the order is wrong.

1 What type of decision does the manager have to make about the customer and why? *(6 marks)*

2 What types of task are being carried out by the staff handling the delivery? Explain your answer. *(9 marks)*

Workplace organisation

What the specification requires

You should understand that businesses have different physical layouts for their offices, work areas and factories. The layouts should match the needs of the business. Each of them has distinct advantages and disadvantages. Technological changes have meant enormous changes to **working practices**, giving businesses and employees opportunities for **flexible working**.

In brief

Businesses are all different, but they all use resources and provide something to customers or clients, and they usually compete with other businesses for sales and customers. There are many factors that can influence how a business sets out its work areas; each option has advantages and disadvantages. Non-traditional working practices can bring great benefits to a business, the management and employees, and this approach is becoming more and more popular.

Revision notes

Working environments are influenced by the needs of the business:

- how work is planned
- how work is organised and scheduled
- how each employee's work area is organised
- where other employees with whom they work regularly are situated
- where the necessary machinery and equipment are located
- whether there are any health and safety concerns

Most office environments are either **open plan** or **cellular**. Each has its own advantages and disadvantages, as shown overleaf.

Speak the language

cellular — traditional small offices

flexible working — offering employees the opportunity to work non-standard hours

open plan — an office layout that consists of a large area separated only by screens and desks

working practices — the way in which the business organises the working patterns of its employees

Open-plan office

Advantages	Disadvantages
■ People work better in teams, can see others doing their work and can communicate better	■ Increased chance that documents might be lost
■ Sharing equipment	■ Theft
■ Managers can supervise more easily	■ Illnesses can easily spread
■ Lighter and more airy environment	■ Some areas less light and warm
■ Cheaper to build, with lower lighting, heating and cleaning costs	■ Too impersonal

Cellular office

Advantages	Disadvantages
■ Quiet and more private	■ Lack of constant supervision
■ Work, documents and equipment in one place	■ Duplicate equipment needed for each office
■ More personal environment	■ People get possessive about their offices
■ Confidentiality and security	■ People are isolated

Fotolia

Open-plan ofices have several advantages and are a popular choice

New practices have changed the way people work. These help to balance workloads and give a better work–life balance, and employees are often more efficient:

■ Hot desks — employees do not have their own work space, but share it and the equipment when they need it. Most employees work elsewhere; this is also known as a virtual office.

■ Home working or teleworking — employees work at home but have access to the business's computer network.

■ Flexitime — employees work core hours (e.g. 10 a.m. to 4 p.m.) and organise the rest of their working day either side of these times.

■ Job sharing — two or more people share the work and the hours of one job role.

■ Shift working — employees may work nights or afternoons and evenings.

■ Compressed hours — employees work 3 or 4 long days each week instead of 5 normal days' work.

Open plan offices are popular and make the best use of space. Communication is always important in the working environment and the layout of the work space may depend on the work flow and the need for face-to-face communication.

In choosing a particular layout, the business has to consider the advantages and disadvantages. In many cases, open plan will be chosen, but rooms will be set aside that can be booked for meetings and private conversations.

Working practices are changing, largely due to advances in technology. This has allowed employees to work in remote locations, but still have access to all the information they need via broadband connection to the business's network. Many changes allow a better work–life balance, a reduction in office space costs and greater efficiency.

Test yourself

Phoenix Plastics Ltd has outgrown its factory and office unit. It has decided to rent a larger unit on the same industrial estate. This will give the business greater opportunity to expand over the next 3 to 5 years. It will also enable the firm to organise its departments and to separate the production area completely from the office area.

1 The sales department wants to set up a call centre. What is this? *(2 marks)*

2 Why is it important for the office space to be separate from the production area of the business? Explain your reasons. *(4 marks)*

3 Suggest and explain the purpose of at least THREE functional departments of a business such as this. *(9 marks)*

Boost your grade Businesses will organise their working environment to maximise the flow of work. It makes sense for the organisation to position close to each other departments or areas of the business that routinely carry out work for, or with, one another. For example, sales might be placed near accounts so that credit checks and queries relating to customer accounts can be handled in an efficient way.

Ergonomics, sustainability and health and safety

What the specification requires

You should understand that **ergonomics** aims to solve practical problems such as preventing avoidable injuries. Health and safety at work is extremely important. Employers and employees have legal responsibilities to maintain a **safe working environment**. You should also remember that businesses are expected to operate in an **environmentally sustainable** manner and not to waste resources.

In brief

Businesses need to be aware of the potential hazards and injuries that could take place in the working environment. Health and safety problems include anything from poorly designed chairs to trailing electrical cables, inadequate cleaning and lack of protective equipment. Businesses have to consider the **social costs and benefits** of their activities and how their operations can affect the environment, both now and in the longer term.

Revision notes

Ergonomics considers the impact of work, equipment and the working environment on employees. This means looking at:
- the job being done
- the equipment
- the physical environment
- the social environment

Speak the language

environmentally sustainable — the activities of the business do not cause avoidable harm to the environment

ergonomics — the science that looks at how people fit with their work

safe working environment — a workplace that is as hazard free as possible

social costs and benefits — the negative and positive impacts a business has on the environment, resources, employees and the general public

The purpose of ergonomics is to reduce negative impacts, accidents, illnesses and injury, and at the same time to increase productivity and performance.

Health and safety issues are very important in the business environment. Businesses have a responsibility to provide a safe working environment and to comply with health and safety laws. Businesses must provide a safe environment for:

- all employees
- anyone visiting the business
- customers of the business
- the general public

It is the responsibility of employers and employees to follow health and safety rules and guidelines (such as the Health and Safety at Work Act 1974). There are other regulations relating to the use of computers, including the Health and Safety (Display Screen Equipment) Regulations 1992. These cover:

- the nature and quality of work stations
- regular breaks for users
- eye examinations
- the size and quality of screens
- keyboards
- work surfaces
- chairs
- the general working environment

Businesses can have positive and negative impacts, known as social benefits and social costs.

Social benefits	Social costs
■ Providing products and services that would not otherwise be available ■ Creating new ideas and inventions ■ Generating wealth through wages and spending ■ Donations to charities	■ Producing emissions and contributing to global warming ■ Water pollution and using harmful chemicals and other toxic items ■ Overusing scarce resources ■ Road congestion and pollution

Businesses now make ethical and environmental aims and objectives a key part of their activities. This can bring them major benefits: customers and investors approve, employees support this approach and the business is seen to be 'green' and committed to being socially responsible. Being socially responsible means:

- only buying from other socially responsible businesses
- fair treatment of employees
- being a good neighbour to the local community
- reducing waste and negative impacts on the environment
- supporting human rights around the world

Health and safety is both a responsibility and a legal requirement for businesses. They must ensure that they do not put employees and others at risk by their activities or working practices.

Ergonomics is a science that seeks to reduce any negative impacts of work on the individual and at the same time to increase efficiency and productivity at work.

Business can have a positive or negative impact on the environment and on the community. They are becoming increasingly socially responsible and aim to eliminate social costs and increase social benefits. A socially responsible business can have a positive image which can help sales and profits and motivate managers and employees.

Test yourself

A business buys its products from a factory in China that employs children. The factory has had a number of accidents and the conditions for employees are very poor. A newspaper has just released photographs of the factory and the general public are shocked.

1 Why might the business have chosen to buy from China? *(2 marks)*

2 What should the business do? Explain your answer. *(5 marks)*

3 Could the business be described as being socially responsible? Explain your answer. *(8 marks)*

Boost your grade In assessing whether a business is socially responsible, look at how far beyond fulfilling its minimum legal obligations the business has got. Being socially responsible does not mean staying within the law. It means being more socially responsible than is legally required.

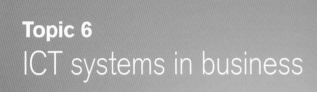

Topic 6
ICT systems in business

What the specification requires

You need to know that there is a range of different **data** types and sources, and that a business needs to collect and process those data accurately. You also need to understand the purposes of different data **input devices** and when they might be used.

In brief

Data sources are documents, electronic communications, and records of meetings, **market research** and other information. All of these have to be collected, collated, analysed and acted on by a business. To make best use of them, the business needs to input the data on to ICT systems, and for this it will use a variety of different devices depending on the types of data and the sources.

Revision notes

Data sources are either **internal** or **external**. Collecting these data gives the business much needed information to base decisions on, or to cope with problems. The main data sources are shown below.

Internal data sources

- Accounts can provide details of transactions, profit or loss, sales trends, spending on salaries and wages.
- Human resources can provide employees' personal details, salaries and wages, training records, employee skills and experience.
- Marketing can provide information on competitors and customers and the effectiveness of advertising.
- Purchasing can provide costs, details of suppliers, spending patterns, orders and stock levels.
- Sales can provide sales figures, customer buying patterns, complaints and problems.
- Production can provide costs, production time and delivery dates.

External data sources

- Government collects information on the economy, population and society.
- Trade information is available specifically about one's particular industry.
- There are businesses that trade in data, collecting them and then selling them on to businesses.
- The European Union and the British government have databases with information.
- Commercial databases collate information.
- Universities carry out research that can be accessed by businesses.

Data input devices are made up of computer hardware supported by software called 'drivers'. Drivers allow the input device to communicate with the computer. The main data input devices are:

- Keyboard — with short-cut keys, numeric keyboards, scrolling keys and special character keys. Most are now either USB, wireless or infrared connected.
- Mouse — a pointing device used to move the cursor, and for manipulating text, drawing, resizing graphics and opening and closing files.
- Other pointing devices — including a stylus (acts like a pen), a touch pad (like a basic keyboard), touch screen (works like the iTouch) and track ball (an ergonomic version of the mouse)
- Scanner — reads text and graphics and displays them on the screen. Text scanners use character recognition software and graphics scanners digitise the image.
- Digital camera — saves the image to a removable storage card, from which the images can be uploaded to a computer.
- Webcam — takes live moving pictures (with sound) which are then displayed on the screens of connected users. This is a two- or more-way communication system.
- Voice recognition software — uses a microphone to capture speech, which then appears in a computer application (such as Word) as text.
- Barcode reader — reads the unique code of products or items using a laser or photocell.
- Optical mark reader — can read marks on documents made by pencil (such as multiple-choice answers).
- Magnetic ink character recognition — reads bank cheques.
- Magnetic strip — a magnetic coating on a plastic card (such as debit card or customer loyalty card) that can hold data.
- Electronic point of sale (EPOS) — essentially a flat-bed barcode reader.
- Electronic fund transfer point of sale (EFTPOS) — a magnetic or chip reader for credit and debit cards in retail outlets.

Ikon/Cadmium

Speak the language

data — any type of information that might be generated by the business or be of value to it from an external source

input devices — hardware and software that allow the user to put information onto a computer

internal and external data — internal data are generated by the business itself and external data may come from any other source outside the business

market research — the systematic investigation of the market, its customers and competition

In a nutshell

A data system is a business's information-processing system. Data sources can be either internal or external. A business will use a range of different input devices to collect information and input it into its computer systems for processing.

Test yourself

1 How does a business make sure that the data sources it is using are to be trusted? *(6 marks)*

2 Suggest FIVE keys that can be found on a keyboard that is designed to aid internet surfing. *(5 marks)*

3 Why might hand-held EFTPOS devices be more secure for banks and users? *(4 marks)*

Boost your grade

It is not just sufficient to collect and store data; the business needs to make use of it. It needs to collate (sort), analyse and then use the data. A business can work out trends, patterns, fashions and other forecasts from the data that it processes. Forecasting is important as it allows the business to try to predict what might happen in the future. In this way, it can prepare for the changes and then respond to them as quickly as possible.

Topic 7
Storage and output

What the specification requires

You will need to understand the purposes and the appropriate use of different **data storage devices** and **data output devices**. It is likely that you will be asked about their use in particular circumstances.

In brief

Businesses need to keep records and be able to retrieve them when needed. In the past, a business would keep physical documents and file them in cabinets. Now it can **digitally store** them, create **databases** and then retrieve those files and either refer to them or print them off if needed. Each business will have its preferred methods, but all of the data must be securely stored and the business must have a range of data output devices to view the data.

Revision notes

Businesses need to keep their records in a safe and secure environment. They will need a system which allows:

- immediate access
- no file to go missing
- archiving of old files, so they do not clutter up the system

The main data storage options are:

- Hard drive — a digitally encoded storage device that records data by magnetising the material in a pattern. It is a sealed unit categorised by its storage capacity, physical size, speed, power consumption and transfer rate.

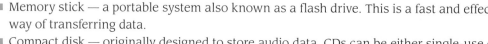

> ### Speak the language
>
> **data output device** — any hardware device that is used to either view or retrieve data
>
> **data storage device** — a drive or a disk that is used to keep data in a safe and secure environment
>
> **database** — a computerised 'filing cabinet' that allows records to be searched, sorted and printed as required
>
> **digitally store** — converting a hard physical copy of a document into a format that can kept on a computer system as a file or an image

- Memory stick — a portable system also known as a flash drive. This is a fast and effective way of transferring data.
- Compact disk — originally designed to store audio data. CDs can be either single-use or used, erased and reused. They are a very cheap option and still common.

- Digital versatile disk — originally designed to store video and sound. DVDs are slowly replacing CDs, as they have higher storage capacity, but they are still more expensive.

A business will also want to access and view data that have been stored; the following are the most common ways of doing this:

- Monitor — including cathode ray tube (CRT), liquid crystal display (LCD) and thin film transistor (TFT). Monitors are categorised by their size, resolution, portability and performance. They can include projectors and laptop or net book screens.
- Printer — including multi-function, inkjet and laser. These are categorised by their speed, quality of print and functionality.
- Communications hardware — including modems and ethernets. These allow connectivity between computers via a network or the internet.

In a nutshell

A business needs to have a wide variety of appropriate hardware to store and then to retrieve, view or print data. The exact choice of the mix of hardware will be dependent on the type of business and the amount of data that has to be collected, analysed, stored and retrieved. Businesses tend to lag behind in the development of new hardware as they may be tied into particular systems or may lack the funds to finance a full replacement and upgrading of the hardware. This means that the systems need to be as upgradeable and replaceable as possible, as changes will tend to happen as older systems wear out or are no longer able to cope with the volume of data.

Ingram

Boost your grade

You need to understand the key purposes and appropriateness of each of the data input and output devices rather than any technical specifications. Most questions will ask you about the main features, advantages and disadvantages of particular devices, or may ask you to recommend ideal devices for particular businesses or circumstances. Remember that data storage needs to be secure and foolproof (with back-ups) and that data output needs to handle data so that they can be viewed, manipulated or communicated over distances.

Test yourself

1 Why might it be important for a business to 'write protect' its documents and data? *(6 marks)*

2 A manufacturer of printers makes a tiny profit from its sales of hardware. It has no option but to discount to remain competitive. Where does the manufacturer make its money and why? *(4 marks)*

3 Why might a business choose to buy a laser printer rather than an inkjet printer? *(5 marks)*

Topic 8
Security of data

What the specification requires

You need to understand that protecting data by making sure that they are secure from external dangers and access is vital to a business. You also need to know that businesses are restricted by law in what they can collect and store, as well as communicate.

In brief

Computers that use Microsoft software are the most vulnerable to **computer viruses**. There are many different types of computer virus and many are **self-replicating** computer programs. Businesses need to protect themselves against these virtual intruders by using **firewalls** and **anti-virus software**. Businesses also need to be aware of guidelines as to what can be stored and how it can be used.

Revision notes

Computer viruses alter the way in which the computer operates without the knowledge or consent of the user of that computer. They are often referred to as 'malicious software' and can infect any part of the computer. They can delete files, damage software programs or leave the computer vulnerable so that someone can access the data on that computer from a remote location. In order to protect computers from these threats, a business will set up a password-protected firewall, which limits access to the computer network from outside users. The business will also run anti-virus software. This aims to disinfect the computer and searches for known viruses. Each virus has a distinct pattern, but it is always a race against time for the anti-virus software to catch up with the latest version of a virus.

Speak the language

anti-virus software — a computer program that searches for and then destroys viruses on infected computers

computer viruses — computer programs that alter the way that the computer operates without the consent of the user of that computer

firewalls — software that acts as a gateway limiting access to a computer network

self-replicating — a virus that can reproduce itself and then infect other computers

Businesses also need to be aware of laws relating to computers and data. Many different businesses hold personal details about individuals, and what can be stored, how it is used and to whom it can be communicated is governed by the Data Protection Act (1998). It is also an offence if someone tries to use data held by a business that they are unauthorised to use. This falls under the Computer Misuse Act (1990). It means that data cannot be:

- altered
- used
- copied
- printed
- moved

In a nutshell

Computer viruses, including Trojan horses and worms, aim to infect, damage, destroy or allow unauthorised access to computer networks. Computer networks are always insecure, as every program has vulnerabilities. Systematically, designers of software try to eliminate these risks. Virus designers are often one step ahead of those who create anti-virus software. New patches and updates are constantly needed to fill security holes in systems.

The key data protection legislation is as follows:

* *Data Protection Act 1998*. All businesses holding data have to register with the Information Commissioner. They are expected to obtain and process data in a fair way and hold it for lawful purposes. They must also show an individual what data they have on them if requested.
* *Computer Misuse Act 1990*. This means that it is an offence to gain unauthorised access to a computer system.

Test yourself

Even major websites are not immune to hackers. Hackers aim to break into computer networks and steal data. Early in 2009 the personal details of 4.5 million people were stolen from an online jobs website. No financial data were taken on this occasion, but many personal details were stolen by the hackers.

1 Suggest FOUR pieces of personal data that hackers might have stolen in this attack. *(4 marks)*

2 Suggest how a website such as this could take immediate action to secure the personal data of users. *(5 marks)*

3 Hackers might use personal details to launch a 'phishing campaign'. What does this mean and what data would the hackers need to have taken? *(6 marks)*

Boost *your grade* Computers are described as 'vulnerable', which relates to their weakness in being able to protect themselves and the data that are held on a network. Vulnerabilities have been found in all operating systems. Software designers have to react immediately if vulnerability is discovered and close it before someone exploits that vulnerability. Businesses need to be vigilant; they need to update their software, install patches and carry out maintenance to protect their systems.

Topic 9
Recruitment and selection

What the specification requires

You will need to know about different types of **employment contract**. You will also need to be aware of the recruitment process, methods of **internal and external recruitment**, and how **job descriptions** and **person specifications** are used.

In brief

Not every employee is a full-time, permanent worker. Some work part time and others have temporary contracts. The contract of employment is a legal document setting out basic rights and responsibilities. Businesses recruit workers using either internal or external methods, and there is a clear recruitment process. Two key documents, the job description and person specification, are used to help define the job role and the type of individual who would be suitable for that role.

Revision notes

Every employee should have a contract of employment, which sets out:

- actual place of work
- job title
- start date
- pay and pay scales
- when wages or salaries will be paid
- other benefits
- normal working hours
- holiday pay and entitlements
- pension details
- arrangements for sickness and maternity leave
- notice period required when leaving

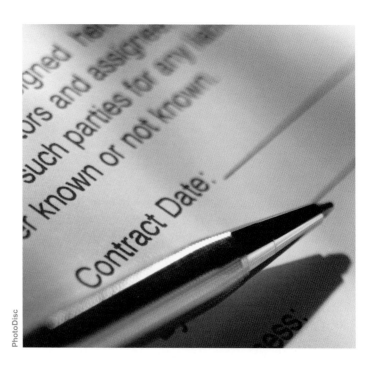

PhotoDisc

The contract is a set of legally binding promises, which clarifies rights and responsibilities. There are a number of different types of employment contract:

- full time — usually up to 40 but perhaps as many as 60 hours per week
- part time — no more than 25 hours per week
- permanent — the job role is long term and may be full or part time
- temporary — the job role is for a limited period only and may be full or part time

Businesses have the option of recruiting either internally or externally. Both have their advantages and disadvantages, but they both need to be well structured and fair, and aim to give the job to the best possible candidate:

- Internal recruitment gives existing employees a chance to gain promotion. The employer knows more about them. It is also a faster and cheaper process.
- External recruitment opens the vacancy to a broader range of candidates, who may have more experience or be better qualified. It also means that the job role of a successful internal candidate does not have to be filled as a result of their promotion.

The normal recruitment method is to:

- advertise the post
- send out details to applicants
- receive, handle and sort applications
- short-list likely candidates
- invite those short-listed for interview
- interview candidates and select the best-suited one

Two key documents are used to help set out the job role: the job description and the person specification.

In a nutshell

A contract of employment is a legally binding document. It is a two-way agreement between the employer and the employee.

Businesses use both internal and external recruitment. Ideally a business needs to fill a post with the best possible candidate and may use a mix of both of these recruitment methods. The external recruitment process can be a long and involved one, including advertising, short-listing, interviewing and then selection of the most suitable candidate.

Job descriptions and person specifications play an important role in the process. The first explains exactly what the job post entails. The second seeks to identify the ideal characteristics, skills and qualifications that someone would need to fulfil those requirements.

Test yourself

Due to falling sales a retail store decides to radically change the contracts of employment of its staff. Most are full-time, permanent workers. They now want to change all of the contracts to part-time, temporary ones. They believe that this would give them more flexibility in bringing employees in when or if they are needed. This will have a huge effect on the staff and they are not happy with the suggestion.

1 What are the key differences between full-time permanent and part-time temporary employees? *(6 marks)*

2 How might the change to part-time, temporary contracts affect the employees' pay and working hours? *(4 marks)*

3 What might have to happen to job descriptions and person specifications? *(5 marks)*

Internal recruitment means that fewer new ideas and skills are brought into an organisation. External recruitment brings new blood into the organisation.

A person specification is an ideal tool for short-listing.

A business can check an application form against the person specification and see how the applicant matches up to the essential and desired skills for that job role.

Topic 10
Training

What the specification requires

You will need to know about different methods of training, including **induction**, **in-house training** and **off-the-job training**. Training is much more than simply passing on skills and knowledge; it is about developing an effective workforce for the future that can be creative, make decisions and work in the most efficient manner.

In brief

Training goes beyond just showing employees how to carry out tasks, or teaching basic skills. Businesses want to develop their employees so that they can make their own judgements and decisions and be more resourceful. Each time they have to choose the best method to achieve this. They also need to be certain that whatever training is offered works and is to the benefit of the business and the individual.

Revision notes

For many employees, training begins with induction. This gives them an opportunity to learn about the business and their own job role. During induction, training needs for that individual may be identified. On a regular basis, however, many employees have **appraisal interviews**. These seek to identify training needs, based on the development of the employee and their current performance. Businesses then need to try to decide what type of training is best suited, both to the business and to the individual:

Appraisal interviews can identify training needs

- work-related training — to obtain key job- or work-related skills or knowledge
- formal training — usually run by external training companies, with a qualification at the end

- informal training — carried out at the workplace and often used by smaller businesses
- distance or internet-based training — this is convenient with no travel costs

A business will also have to decide whether it is more appropriate to offer training in the workplace or away from the workplace:

- *On-the-job training.* This can be either formal or informal. It can also be skills-based or knowledge-based. It allows the employee to develop through training while they are working. This means everything they learn is directly related to their job role and to the workplace.
- *Off-the-job training.* This means sending the employee away from the workplace, for half a day, a day or an extended period. The training will usually be carried out by external experts. The disadvantage is that the training may not relate directly either to the employee's job role or to the type of work carried out by the business. It does, however, usually lead to a formal qualification.

Many businesses use a mixture of on- and off-the job training. NVQs are good examples of on-the-job training where the skills of an employee are recognised. Any gaps in their skills or knowledge can be filled by off-the-job training programmes.

On-the-job training allows employees to learn while they are working

In a nutshell

Training is not just about passing on skills and knowledge; it is also about developing employees. A business needs to identify the type of training that is needed and then decide how it should be delivered. It then needs to look at the training and evaluate it to see if it has been effective. Training can begin at induction and continue throughout the career of an employee. Effective training means not only developing the individual, but also bringing new skills, knowledge and expertise to the business itself.

Test yourself

Harper's Hardware Stores has decided to set up its own management academy. It is a rapidly growing chain and wants to create a training programme that will identify its key managers and potential leaders of the future. The business already has well-trained staff and takes recruitment and training very seriously. The training programme begins at induction, with an intensive 12-week course. It is an in-house training programme. After this the managers are posted to one of the branches, where they work for another 12 weeks. At the end of this they have an appraisal interview, where additional training is identified and authorised.

1 Why is it important for a business such as this to focus its training budget on its key employees? *(6 marks)*

2 Why do you think the business has structured the first 24 weeks in this way? What does the business hope to achieve? *(9 marks)*

Boost your grade Induction training is very important because it is a method of getting across the business's goals, objectives and practices. In order for induction to work, it needs to be well-organised. Induction is far more than skills training. It is also vital in helping employees settle into the business and to be effective in their new job role from the very beginning.

Topic 11
Rewarding staff

What the specification requires

You will need to know about the different methods of **remuneration**, how to make simple pay calculations and about other forms of **financial rewards** and **non-financial rewards**.

In brief

Pay is only one aspect of the overall reward package offered to employees by employers. Training, greater responsibility and a range of non-financial rewards are all offered. Employees are usually paid either wages or salaries, but some are paid on an hourly basis, while others receive pay for every item or task that they complete. Some employees are also paid overtime, bonuses and **commission**. Employees do not receive their full pay. Deductions, which may include tax, national insurance, pension contributions, trade union subscriptions and charitable donations, all come out of employees' gross pay to produce their net pay.

Revision notes

Rewarding staff does not just mean offering a competitive salary or wage. Training, responsibility and non-financial rewards are very important as part of the overall package. Employees receive their pay in a number of different ways:

- As a wage — paid weekly, sometimes in cash. It will usually be the number of hours worked multiplied by the hourly rate plus any overtime payments.
- As a salary — paid monthly, as a twelfth of the yearly pay of the employee.

Employees may be paid weekly or monthly

Some employees are paid on a slightly different basis:

- Piece-rate — instead of being paid for the number of hours worked, they are paid on a piece rate for the number of items they have made or tasks they have completed.
- Bonus — in addition to their wage or salary, they may receive a bonus because either they or the business have achieved a goal or objective.
- Comission — in addition to a low salary, some will receive commission, which is a percentage of the total value of the sales that they have generated.
- Performance-related pay — instead of having a set salary, the employee will receive additional payments as long as they manage to achieve specific goals.

In working out pay, the following takes place:

- An employee on a salary is paid one-twelfth of their total yearly pay each month.
- An employee on a wage is paid for the hours worked multiplied by the hourly rate of pay plus any overtime hours at that overtime hourly rate.
- The employer then deducts from this gross pay figure the income tax, national insurance and other deductions, such as pension contributions, charity donations and subscriptions. This produces the employee's net pay.

Non-financial rewards add to the overall package offered to an employee and these can include:

- subsidised meals, drinks and travel
- a company car or essential car user's allowance
- work expenses
- a discount on purchases made from the business
- reduced loans or mortgages
- health insurance

Speak the language

commission — a small percentage of the total value of sales generated by an employee, which makes up the bulk of their pay package

financial reward — pay, or any other monetary-based reward, such as a pension, bonus, commission or overtime payment

non-financial reward — any part of a package offered to an employee that is not pay-based, such as subsidised travel, company car or reduced loans and mortgages

remuneration — this is a term used to describe all types of pay, whether they be a wage or a salary

Fotolia

In a nutshell

When businesses reward staff they offer a package of financial and non-financial incentives. An employee does not receive their gross pay; they receive their net pay, which has been calculated by deducting income tax, national insurance and subscriptions or donations. Employees may value non-financial rewards, such as training, greater responsibility, and the opportunity to acquire skills and knowledge and to receive fringe benefits or incentives, almost as much as financial ones. Some businesses also offer very generous pension plans.

Test yourself

A business receives an order for 1,000 products. It will sell them to the customer for £10 each. The cost of the materials to make them will be £4,000. The business will need to offer 20 employees 5 hours of overtime each to make sure that the work is completed.

1 What do you understand by the term 'overtime'? *(2 marks)*

2 If the business wants to make £3,000 from the deal to make the products for the customer, how much per hour can it offer the 20 workers as their overtime payment? *(8 marks)*

3 If the employees on average lose 40% of their gross pay, how much will each of them earn as net pay for doing the overtime for this job? *(5 marks)*

Boost your grade Bonuses are a very effective way to reward employees for their contribution in helping a business achieve its aims and objectives. In the past, many businesses offered generous pension schemes, which were based on the salaries of their employees while they were in work. These have proved to be extremely expensive and difficult to fund and are now becoming rarer and more sought after by employees.

Topic 12
Employment rights and responsibilities

What the specification requires

You will need to be aware of **legislation** that has an effect on employment **rights and responsibilities**.

In brief

Although most businesses will have policies on how they handle their relationships with employees, there are key rights and responsibilities that are enforced by law. The law is there to make sure that minimum standards and requirements are placed on employees and employers and the relationship between the two of them. One main area relates to **discrimination**. Various laws have been introduced in order to eliminate discrimination and to try to ensure **equal opportunities** for all.

Revision notes

Legislation refers to laws, regulations and directives that have been approved by the UK parliament. Some, often referred to as regulations and directives, are in fact European Union laws. In most cases, the UK has decided to apply these and make them law. There are many minimum legal requirements, relating to, for example:

- equal opportunities
- working hours and overtime
- pay
- harassment, victimisation and bullying
- disciplinary action
- leave and absence
- maternity, paternity and adoption

Good employers have policies in place which exceed the minimum legal requirements

Over the years, a number of laws have come into force to try to make sure that everyone, regardless of their age, gender, religion, nationality or disability, is treated in the same, equal manner:

- Equal Pay Act 1970 — aims to ensure that both men and women receive the same pay for broadly the same work.
- National Minimum Wage Act 1998 — provides a legal right to receive at least a minimum hourly rate of pay from an employer.
- Sex Discrimination Act 1975 — outlaws discrimination on the grounds of gender, marital status or sexual orientation.
- Race Relations Act 1976 — makes it unlawful to discriminate on the basis of someone's skin colour, ethnic background, nationality, religion or belief.
- Disability Discrimination Acts 1995 and 2005 — require employers to make reasonable adjustments to working conditions to allow those with a disability to work for them.

Anti-discrimination laws provide equal opportunities for all

Fotolia

In recent years, it has also become unlawful to discriminate on the grounds of age. A good business and a responsible employer will do far more than the basic minimum. They will offer a far better range of rights and take greater responsibility in handling their relationships with their employees. There is no law related to training, the use of company facilities and other aspects, but good employers will make them part of their minimum standards.

In a nutshell

There are laws that govern the relationship between employers and employees, setting out the minimum rights and responsibilities. Laws can only impose minimum standards; good employers exceed these minimum standards. It is unlawful for an employer to discriminate against an employee on a number of different grounds, such as their gender or age. They can expect to be prosecuted. The rules and regulations are there to ensure that equality of opportunity is guaranteed.

Test yourself

Beatrice is unhappy. She is 64 years old and will be 65 in a month's time. She has just been told by her manager that she is too old to work for the business any more and that they expect her to retire before her next birthday. Beatrice is particularly unhappy because there are four people older than her working for the business. They are all in senior positions and they are all male.

1 Is Beatrice being reasonable about this? What rights do you think she has? Explain your answer. *(10 marks)*

2 Suggest how the business should deal with this situation. *(5 marks)*

Boost your grade

In theory, everyone who starts working for an employer is entitled to a written contract within 2 months. This should lay out all of the basics, including pay, working hours, holiday entitlement, notice period and information on disciplinary procedures. The contract is an agreement and a legally binding one. It will refer to legislation, but it will not list all the laws. When the contract is signed, both sides agree to be bound by it, accepting that they have rights and also responsibilities to one another and the law.

Communication

Topic 13
Communication

What the specification requires

You will need to understand the importance of communication and the key benefits of **effective communication**.

In brief

Effective communication is absolutely essential in business. Information flows in, out and around a business every day. All of it needs to be checked, read, understood, communicated to others and acted upon. This includes **internal communication** and **external communication**. In each case, the most appropriate type of communication needs to be chosen. The benefits of effective communication are clear. It can make the difference between profit and loss, success and failure.

Revision notes

Communication has two key purposes:
- acquiring information — this is about collecting, noticing and checking all types of internal and external communication
- disseminating information — passing on information to those who need it to do their job, solve a problem or take a decision

In order for communication to work it needs to be:
- *Appropriate*. This means choosing the right type of communication, such as a letter, an e-mail, a report or simply a conversation.
- *Clear*. There should be no room for confusion and little doubt as to what is meant by the communication. This means choosing the right language and, perhaps, making it as simple as possible.

Speak the language

effective communication — this means choosing the most appropriate form of communication, which is clear and accurate.

external communication — communication with those from outside the organisation, such as customers, other businesses and groups

internal communication — any form of communication between those that work inside the organisation

verbal and written communication — verbal communication is the spoken word in a conversation, meeting or telephone call; written communication includes letters, e-mails and reports.

- *Accurate.* All the facts and figures need to be checked to see if they are correct. This means checking figures, times, dates, names and other facts to ensure that they are correct.
- *The right image and tone.* The image is a reflection of the way that the business wants to appear, particularly to those outside the business. The tone is the approach that is adopted in what is said or written and is a major part of image.

PhotoDisc

The benefits of good communication mean that everyone who needs to know about something is informed. It also means that they are up-to-date. Businesses use a mix of **verbal and written communication** to interact with individuals within the organisation and individuals, groups and other businesses from outside the organisation. Businesses might use:

- e-mails, newsletters, bulletins or notice boards, as well as meetings to keep their employees informed
- advertisements, letters, brochures, leaflets and other publicity material to keep those outside the organisation informed

Communication takes place on a daily basis, both within and outside the organisation. Telephone calls, e-mails, letters, faxes and a host of other documents are used. All of these help to ensure that people are well informed and that they can make the right decision when they need to make it.

In a nutshell

A business will have to choose the most appropriate way of communicating and ensure that its communication is clear and accurate, and that it represents the business in terms of image and tone. Making sure that everyone who needs information is made aware of it is vital if the correct decisions are to be made at the right time, using the most up-to-date facts and figures.

Test yourself

Gary runs the warehouse for a builders' merchant. He only started a month ago. Everyone was too busy to show him around or tell him how anything worked. Yesterday a truck load of bricks was sent to Brixham instead of Brixton and today a lorry load of cement turned up at a home for the elderly instead of Elderly Homes Ltd in the next town.

1 What are the consequences of the mistakes that Gary has been making? *(6 marks)*

2 How should the business deal with the situation? *(9 marks)*

Boost your grade For truly effective communication there needs to be:

- clarity — no room for confusion
- conciseness — only include the bare facts
- appropriate language — avoid using complex words and try to support the words with tables, graphs and other images
- brevity — be brief, use subheadings and only include the important facts
- no jargon — avoid using technical terms unless it is absolutely essential

Topic 14
Communication systems

What the specification requires

You will need to understand the **process of communication** and to be aware of the different **channels of communication**. You will also need to know that there are four major **methods of communication** and when these are likely to be used.

In brief

There is a standard communication model, consisting of the sender, receiver, message and medium. There are different channels of communication, ranging from formal to informal and confidential to non-confidential. There are also four key methods of communication: oral, visual, written and pictorial.

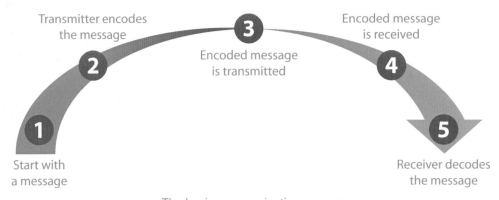

The basic communication process

Revision notes

Although there are many different ways in which businesses can collect, share and pass on information, all of them are based on a simple communication model, as can be seen in the diagram.

The sender prepares the message and chooses the communication method that is most appropriate. They then send or transmit the message to the person it is intended to reach, known as the receiver. When the receiver gets the message, they have to understand what the message is about and what they are expected to do with it. They then respond and in responding they give **feedback** to the sender, which tells them that they have understood the message.

There are various channels of communication:

- *Formal and informal.* Formal communications include business letters and contracts of employment. Informal communications include face-to-face discussions and telephone conversations.
- *Internal and external.* Some types of communication are more appropriate for internal use, such as meetings, memoranda and notices. Others are more appropriate for external communication, such as letters and e-mails.
- *Confidential and non-confidential.* Confidential information may include sensitive information that is only intended for the receiver. Non-confidential communication can be viewed by othcrs.
- *Urgent and non-urgent.* Some communications are given priority because they need to be dealt with immediately, while others are more routine.

The four key methods of communication are:

- oral communication — face-to-face or remote conversation
- visual communication — including face-to-face, notice boards and videoconferencing
- written communication — including e-mails and letters
- pictorial communication — where the information is displayed as a chart, drawing or graph

Individuals read a great deal into the gestures and facial expressions of people. This key aspect of communication occurs in face-to-face communication. This type of communication is also appropriate therefore in videoconferencing, where both sound and vision are used. Many people also believe that non-verbal communication (also known as 'body language') tells us far more about the person and the message than the actual message itself.

Speak the language

channels of communication — this is about recognising and then using the right way to communicate information based on the nature of the information and who the receiver is

feedback — a response or confirmation that a message has been received and understood

methods of communication — broadly these are oral, visual, written and pictorial, although some communication methods are a mixture of all of these

process of communication — a loop in which individuals constantly send messages to and receive messages from one another

A presentation uses a mixture of communication methods

The communication process should be seen as a closed loop, where the sender communicates with the receiver and then the receiver communicates with the sender, either to feed back or confirm that they have received and understood the message. The choice of medium or communication method is very important, as it needs to take account of the fact that the communication may be confidential, only for internal use or urgent. Broadly there are just four key types of communication method: oral, visual, written and pictorial.

Test yourself

Allan has made a terrible mistake. He has been working for a company now for 5 years and the only thing he does not like about it is the long commute to work. He likes the job and the people. Allan decides to apply for another job at a business much closer to his home. He says his goodbyes to his friends at work and begins his new job. Before lunch on the first day, he knows he has made this dreadful mistake. The job is nothing like he was expecting, no one has talked to him and he does not know what he is supposed to be doing and whether the work he has been given will even last him the week. He tells his new boss that he has made the wrong decision and that he is going to ring his old employer and ask for his old job back. His new boss tells him to leave immediately — he has been fired.

Boost your grade The full communication process involves sorting out the message, encoding it, choosing the right medium and sending it, and the receiver decoding and feeding back to the sender, which in turn generates another message from the original sender.

1 What communication problems may have occurred before Allan took the job to have caused this problem in the first place? *(8 marks)*

2 How should Allan have handled the situation? *(7 marks)*

Topic 15
Communication systems and barriers

What the specification requires

You should be able to choose the right communication medium in specific situations. You will need to be able to describe the key features of communication media and need to be aware that there are often **barriers to communication**, which can cause confusion and misunderstanding.

In brief

There are a number of different potential communication media, including:

- telephone
- face-to-face
- **teleconferencing**
- memoranda
- letters
- financial documents
- advertisements
- e-mail
- **videoconferencing**
- **electronic bulletin boards**
- drawings, graphs and charts

Each of them has key features and is more or less appropriate in different situations. Often there are communication problems and barriers to communication. These need to be overcome in order for the message to be clearly understood.

Revision notes

Each time an individual or a business wants to make a communication with another individual, group or business, it needs to choose the most appropriate medium. This means taking account of the message itself and the audience or receiver. There are a number of key options:

- telephone communication — ideal for most informal communications and some formal communication

The most appropriate medium should be chosen for the message

- face-to-face communication — appropriate in most internal communication situations, which can be formal or informal, and also ideal in most cases when dealing with customers
- teleconferencing — allows more than two individuals in remote locations to have a telephone conversation and may be ideal for internal and some external situations
- memoranda — usually just an internal, formal or informal communication
- letters — usually a formal communication with those outside the business
- financial documents — some are prepared for internal use only, although limited companies need to publish certain financial documents in a fixed format
- advertisements — designed for external individuals and groups
- e-mail — depending on the format chosen, these can either be formal or informal and are widely used internally and externally by businesses
- videoconferencing — essentially an upgraded version of teleconferencing, including sound and vision, which can be used for formal meetings or informal conversations
- electronic bulletin boards — online communication systems, which can be restricted to internal use or open to all
- drawings, graphs and charts — these can usually be seen as an additional way of enhancing information and making complicated information easier to understand

There are often potential communication problems, including:
- lack of information
- problems with the relationship between the sender and the receiver
- faulty systems (such as a breakdown in procedures or a poor mobile phone signal)

Fotolia

- muddled messages
- stereotyping — assuming that everyone has the same level of understanding
- choosing the wrong channel — trying to tell somebody something complicated when it should be written down
- use of complicated language or jargon
- interruptions and distractions
- poor listening skills of the receiver
- the receiver not giving feedback

In a nutshell

Methods of communication break down broadly into oral and written. Oral communications include telephone, face-to-face and teleconferencing. Written communications include memos and letters. These can be supported by visual communications, including videoconferencing and electronic notice boards. To support written communication in particular, graphical communication is used. Individuals and businesses need to be aware that there are barriers to effective communication and need to consider the medium used and the audience for which the message is intended.

Test yourself

It was the end of a very busy and tiring day for Jack. He must have answered the telephone at least 30 times and had been running around the office all day dealing with customer queries. It was 4.55 p.m. and he was looking forward to going home when the phone rang again. It was Mr O'Keefe. Without thinking, Jack said, 'Would you mind calling back in the morning? We are closed.' He hung up. A second later the phone rang again and Mr O'Keefe demanded to speak to Jack's boss.

1 How should Jack have greeted Mr O'Keefe? *(2 marks)*

2 What was wrong with Jack's reaction to the phone call? *(4 marks)*

3 What impression did Jack give Mr O'Keefe of his attitude to him as a valued customer? *(4 marks)*

4 Suggest how Jack's boss might react and why. *(5 marks)*

Boost your grade The best communication method is the one that is most appropriate to the audience. Good communication will use as many human senses as possible, especially hearing and sight (including body language). To ensure that communications are effective, businesses need to be creative and find the best ways to get their messages across. They will vary the channels and techniques and will try to avoid miscommunication.

Topic 16
The importance of ICT in business

What the specification requires

You will need to understand the key characteristics and uses of **application software**, including word processing, presentations, spreadsheets, databases, graphics and desktop publishing.

In brief

All businesses are reliant on information and communication technology (ICT). They need to balance the investment costs and maintenance costs with the advantages that ICT can bring them. Businesses use a broad range of application software, for tasks from basic word processing to the creation of electronic databases and the manipulation of figures using spreadsheet software.

Revision notes

The key benefits of ICT are:
- Lower hardware and software costs have made ICT more widespread.
- Communication is faster and more efficient.
- Electronic files can be shared.
- Data can be processed more quickly.
- **Standardised documents** can be created.
- Even simple websites can attract new customers.
- **E-commerce** opens up the world as a market.

However, there are some barriers:
- The business might not be able to justify the expense.
- The business's customers may prefer face-to-face communication.

Desktop publishing software is widely used in the publishing industry

- The business might lack necessary skills and knowledge about what to buy and how to use it.
- There may be worries about development and maintenance costs.
- There might be a poor internet connection in the business's area.
- There may be worries about trust and security.

The key types of application software and their main uses are:

- word processing — creating templates, generating documents and **mail merge**
- presentation software — creating templates and layouts incorporating graphics and text
- database software — collecting and storing information and selecting specific information
- spreadsheet software — collecting, ordering and making calculations using numerical data and assisting businesses to predict financial changes
- graphics — used to improve the presentation of information and to produce more professional-looking documents
- desktop publishing software — to produce professional newsletters and stationery without the need to use a designer

Speak the language

application software — a software package that is designed to perform a specific function or series of functions

e-commerce — offering products or services over the internet, allowing the whole transaction to be completed online

mail merge — combining lists of names and addresses with a standard letter or other document

standardised documents — templates that set out precisely how each type of document should look or be presented

In a nutshell

ICT has become a vital part of a business's day-to-day operations. It is used for both basic and more complex functions. The key benefit of ICT is the improved efficiency and communication opportunities it offers for the business. Some businesses are reluctant to use ICT due to costs, lack of knowledge or concerns that their customers will not welcome new approaches. Key application software is fairly universal. Many businesses use the Microsoft Office suite, which has become the industry standard. A key advantage of using a suite of application software is that it is possible to import and export material from one application to another. Not only does ICT allow businesses to produce more professional documents and procedures, but it also allows documents and data to be shared, analysed and amended as required.

Many businesses use the Microsoft Office suite

The use of ICT and e-commerce varies from industry to industry. In tourism, for example, although the market is dominated by several large businesses, smaller businesses can still compete by offering their services through websites and generating direct sales. In retailing, a large number of very small businesses are able to compete with larger retail chains because they can offer products and services over the internet that the larger businesses do not offer. ICT does not just help improve sales and communication between a business and its customers; it also helps along the whole supply chain, allowing businesses and their suppliers to work more closely together and to communicate in a more efficient way.

Test yourself

A retail store that sells clothes made by small-scale designers has always relied on face-to-face communication with its customers. It has found that customers prefer to see the clothes and try them before they buy. As a result, the store has been reluctant to create a website and to offer any of its products over the internet. One problem is that some of the designers that supply the store are offering their products direct over the internet.

1 What possible benefits might the retail store gain in developing a website with e-commerce? *(5 marks)*

2 How might the business use mail merge to inform existing customers of the launch of a new range of designer clothes? *(4 marks)*

3 How might the business use a database to help it organise its customer records? *(6 marks)*

Topic 17
The internet

What the specification requires

You will need to understand that there are different computer networks and how **local area networks** (intranet) and **wide area networks** (internet) are used.

In brief

As businesses grow, they may set up a **computer network**. The usual first step is to establish a local area network (LAN). This connects workstations, printers and servers, allowing shared access and file exchange. The LAN will have internet access. If the business is operating on more than one site, it will need a wide area network (WAN). This can connect several local area networks together. Businesses may also need **storage area networks** (SAN), where files and data can be stored and accessed.

Revision notes

A computer network allows the sharing of:
- application software
- files and databases
- information
- peripherals, including scanners and printers

A local area network (LAN) connects workstations, printers and servers

Fotolia

Speak the language

computer network — two or more computers that are connected together, by either cable or wireless, and also connected to peripherals

local area network — a high-speed data network designed to cover a relatively small area

storage area network — a high-speed, special-purpose network designed for the storage of data

wide area network — a computer network that allows two or more LANs to be connected to one another

Computers in a network can be connected either by cabling or by using a wireless system

A LAN is a basic computer network, with two or more computers connected and files stored centrally. These computers can be connected either by cabling or by using a wireless system. Wireless networks are cheaper to install, but signal quality can often be a problem. Some buildings have black spots where no signal is available. Some wireless networks are slower and it is also difficult to keep the network secure, as wireless transmissions can be intercepted. Despite the drawbacks, when businesses install networks for the first time wireless is the usual choice, as it allows greater flexibility and eliminates the need for cabling. Peripherals can also be positioned wherever they are most convenient for all users.

If the business only shares its network internally, this is known as an intranet. If the business allows the network to be accessed remotely then it is known as an extranet. WANs are an option for businesses operating on more than one site. Central servers are connected over a telecommunications network; this is still safe and secure. Storage area networks are high-speed, special-purpose networks for storage. Additional storage can be added as the business grows.

The vast majority of businesses are connected to the internet via broadband or cable services. This allows them to use the internet for e-mails, instant messaging and the exchange of data and information. The internet is a dynamic system and the routers and servers used always try to find the best connection. A business will use a firewall to protect its network and will restrict access to particular parts of the network by using passwords and other security devices.

In a nutshell

A computer network allows the sharing of applications and data, and streamlines communication. Local area networks are the first step in building a computer network. They can be either cable or wireless connected. If a business allows its network to be accessed remotely, this is known as an extranet. WANs are designed to connect several LANs together. Businesses can also use SANs as their key storage facility. The vast majority of businesses are connected to the internet, allowing greater communication with customers and suppliers. They can then cooperate with other businesses and exchange data using common software.

Test yourself

A new business has just moved into a purpose-built suite of offices. It has 20 people working in the office and another 10 in remote locations around the country. The business wants to be able to share data throughout the office and allow its remote workers access to the computer network. It also wants to set up access for customers and suppliers to certain parts of the network. The business wants the system to be capable of expansion.

1 Would a wireless network be more efficient and flexible for the business than a cabled one? Explain your answer. *(6 marks)*

2 How could the business allow its remote employees to access the organisation's intranet? *(4 marks)*

3 Apart from the budget, what other questions should the business ask itself about its network? *(5 marks)*

Boost your grade An intranet allows internet access, but external users cannot access it from outside the network. An intranet would need its own extranet to provide controlled access from outside. Businesses need to think about the requirements of their network, including regular tasks, expansion, equipment needs, budget and who will need access to it.

The internet: opportunities and threats

What the specification requires

You will need to understand the ways in which businesses use the internet, and the key advantages and disadvantages, including the opportunities and risks of using the internet and e-commerce.

In brief

The primary uses of the internet as far as businesses are concerned are:
- creating websites
- offering e-commerce
- improved communications
- access to global and international markets
- marketing opportunities
- reduced **stockholding**
- a shorter **supply chain**
- ability to be more **footloose**

Revision notes

Even the smallest business can use the internet to reach a global marketplace. A business can design a website and offer products and services to customers throughout the world, around the clock, and then allow customers to place orders and pay for purchases online. Not all businesses opt for an e-commerce website; some simply explain the products and services that the business offers, or the website simply complements its normal operations. Internet-based businesses are not like conventional shops; they do not have to be based on the high street. This means that they can locate in a cheap area, as their shop window is their website. Secure, online transactions allow customers to pay for products and services without worrying about security issues.

> **Speak the language**
>
> **footloose** — a business that does not have to locate itself in any particular place and may choose a cheaper location or a location that suits the owners of the business
>
> **stockholding** — the products held in storage by a business in anticipation that they will be sold to customers
>
> **supply chain** — all of the businesses and the processes involved in transforming raw materials into finished goods ready for sale to customers
>
> **traffic** — the number of unique visitors to a particular website

Businesses may also use a number of different features on their websites to improve **traffic**. These include:

- discussion forums
- polls and voting
- weblogs
- news feeds
- feedback
- subscription forms
- online order and delivery tracking

Although there are many opportunities offered by the internet, there are also risks, as identified below.

Internet opportunities	Internet risks
▪ Global visibility ▪ Simplified internal and external communication ▪ Ability to gather information ▪ Ability to update instantly ▪ Keep stock levels low ▪ Automated payment systems ▪ Lower-cost location	▪ Hostile or critical publicity ▪ Dealing with parts of the world that the business has little knowledge about ▪ Vulnerability to hostile attack ▪ Hackers ▪ Denial of service attacks ▪ Dealing with increased demand ▪ Inability to keep up with the latest technology

Fotolia

The internet gives businesses access to global markets and the opportunity to increase sales

The internet and e-commerce allow businesses to inform their customers quickly about the business and its products. They also allow customers to place orders and to make online purchases. The internet helps businesses, regardless of their size, to be more competitive in the global market. Businesses can offer their products and services around the world all year round, hopefully increasing their market share. However, they can expose themselves to threats: not only is there the cost of setting up and maintaining the website, but they are also exposed to increased competition. Operating worldwide also means having to have 24-hour customer service. Added to this, they also run the risk of unauthorised access and the potential theft of confidential customer data.

Boost your grade

Online businesses increasingly use interactive customisation. This allows them to collect data on each unique user of the website and then customise the look of the website to match that customer's usual behaviour and interests. Businesses need to update their websites on a very regular basis; they use content management software to enable a number of people to add, delete or update content. Businesses now have to provide websites that can be viewed not only on computers or laptops, but also on mobile phones and personal digital assistants. This means that websites have to be enormously flexible, but it also means that customers can view the website almost anywhere. Businesses need to be careful about how much they spend in establishing their online presence; many new businesses fail in their first year because they overestimate how much money the website will generate.

Test yourself

Bradwell Global Travel Ltd is a small, local travel agency. It primarily sells direct to customers face-to-face or on the telephone. The owners are worried that, as they do not have a website, or e-mail, they are at an enormous disadvantage compared with their larger competitors. Their competitors use computers and electronic communications every day to deal with their suppliers, including airlines and tour operators. The owners are also concerned that it will cost too much money to set up a website and that it would not guarantee them access to a broader customer base.

1 Why might this sort of business opt for a static website in the first instance?   *(5 marks)*

2 The business is seriously considering offering a broader range of services to a wider range of customers. What features would be necessary for its new website?   *(10 marks)*

Section tests

Case study 1

Carelocal Ltd

Carelocal Ltd provides home help and assistance for the elderly, terminally ill or housebound. It offers a range of basic care, including preparing meals, companionship and cleaning. It also arranges shopping to be delivered and transport for hospital appointments for its clients. The business has six shareholders and employs 42 people. It has a human resource manager, an accountant, one person who deals with marketing and sales, and one customer service manager, and the rest of the staff are involved in dealing directly with the customers. The business operates out of an office unit, but does not have very much in the way of stock, although it does have three minibuses. Each of the care

Fotolia

workers uses their own car and the running costs are paid for by the business. Each care worker has a mobile telephone and a laptop computer for communication and to receive their daily rotas and workloads. The business carefully selects suitably qualified employees, using external recruitment. It offers in-house training and the opportunity to obtain NVQs. The business uses ICT for a number of purposes, including the generation of invoices for customers, maintaining a full database of all customers past and present, and staff wages. The company has a website, but it is primarily used as a brochure for its services and it does not have an e-commerce facility, although the business does have an e-mail address.

AO1–AO2 questions

1 What is the role of a human resources manager? *(2 marks)*

2 What is meant by the term 'stock'? *(2 marks)*

3 What do you understand by the term 'external recruitment'? *(2 marks)*

4   What is an invoice? *(2 marks)*

5   Suggest FIVE details that might be kept on a database of customers. *(5 marks)*

6   Apart from the shareholders, suggest FOUR other likely stakeholders of the business. *(4 marks)*

7   Suggest a piece of application software that would be useful to the accountant. *(2 marks)*

8   Suggest THREE possible aims and objectives of this type of business. *(3 marks)*

9   Suggest at least one job role that is missing and explain your answer. *(5 marks)*

10 Suggest why training might be important to all the business's employees. *(5 marks)*

AO3 questions

1   Carelocal Ltd is a medium-sized business. Suggest how it might judge its success as a business. *(6 marks)*

2   The business recognises that it needs an administrator. What is an administrator and how could this role assist the business? *(8 marks)*

3   Some of the care workers also operate as supervisors to less experienced care workers. Why might this be an advantage and how might they be able to improve the business's operations? *(8 marks)*

4   The care workers work in very different working environments, but they still need to be aware of their legal responsibilities, as does the employer. Suggest how health and safety legislation might apply. *(8 marks)*

5   Identify and explain TWO likely data input and TWO likely data output devices that might be used by the business. *(8 marks)*

6   The business is likely to hold some very sensitive and confidential information about its customers. How should it seek to protect these data? *(8 marks)*

7   Why might the recruitment and selection of staff for the job role of a care worker be especially important? What additional checks might have to be made? *(6 marks)*

8   The care workers are paid on an hourly basis. In addition they must submit their travel expenses every month. They receive free medical care and free life insurance, paid for by the business. Which of these are fringe benefits? Explain your answer. *(6 marks)*

9   Why might it not be appropriate for the business to have anything more than a very basic website? Explain your answer. *(8 marks)*

10 Explain why effective communication in a business such as this is vitally important. *(8 marks)*

Case study 2

Forrester Sales and Marketing Ltd

Forrester Sales and Marketing Ltd sells wooden benches, chairs and tables. For many years it operated out of a series of cellular offices in its old premises. It had a large sales department and most of the sales were achieved by making telephone calls to potential customers. These would then be followed up by visits by sales representatives. The business has now moved to a newer building and has an open-plan office. Sales representatives only come to the main building three or four times a year for sales conferences and meetings, but they have an area set aside for them to hot desk if they need to. The business has become reliant on technology to improve its communications and sales, and many sales are in fact now generated through its dynamic website, which is constantly updated by the website team. The business pays a basic salary. On top of this, it pays overtime, bonuses and commission to its sales staff. It also offers a range of fringe benefits, including cars, medical care and life insurance to its field sales teams. All staff are trained to use a broad range of application software and are also trained in sales techniques and customer service. The sales teams keep in touch by supplying detailed logs of visits that they have made to customers, along with information on orders and the reactions of customers to the products. This is then passed on to appropriate departments in the business to deal with particular problems or issues as they arise. The business has an excellent reputation for customer service and for communications with customers. It has recently added online payment systems to its website so that orders can be made direct by members of the public. The business also makes use of videoconferencing and teleconferencing, and encourages home working, teleworking and flexitime.

Ingram

AO1–AO2 questions

1 Suggest THREE aspects that you might find on a dynamic website. *(3 marks)*

2 What is meant by the term 'bonus'? *(2 marks)*

3 What is meant by the term 'commission'? *(2 marks)*

4 What type of software might be used by the sales teams to supply logs of their visits? *(2 marks)*

5 Give TWO advantages of being able to offer products direct to the public. *(4 marks)*

6 What is hot desking? *(2 marks)*

7 What is a cellular office? *(2 marks)*

8 What is meant by the term 'flexitime'? *(2 marks)*

9 Distinguish between videoconferencing and teleconferencing. *(6 marks)*

10 Suggest THREE types of application software that are likely to be used by a broad range of staff in this type of business. *(6 marks)*

AO3 questions

1 Distinguish between cellular and open-plan offices. *(8 marks)*

2 Why might a dynamic website be ideal for this type of business? *(8 marks)*

3 If a sales representative is paid a basic salary of £10,000 per year and receives 5% commission on sales of £600,000, what is their average monthly gross pay for that year? *(8 marks)*

4 Explain why it is important for the sales team to inform head office about visits to customers. *(8 marks)*

5 What are the advantages of ensuring that the sales representatives remain in their regions, rather than operating from a central office? *(8 marks)*

6 Suggest which departments might be involved in dealing with a customer complaint. Explain your answer. *(8 marks)*

7 What are the advantages of offering fringe benefits to employees? *(8 marks)*

8 Why might it be important for the business to provide training in sales techniques and customer service? *(8 marks)*

9 Why is the reputation of a business such as this extremely important for its long-term success? *(8 marks)*

10 How might a business such as this use ICT to ensure continued growth and success? *(8 marks)*

Case study 3

Anderson Toys Ltd

Anderson Toys' expansion has been a disaster from start to finish. It started as three partners, all making handmade wooden toys for the local market. They designed a simple website and began selling their toys around the world. Demand got too great for the three of them to cope with, so they took on eight other people, expanded the website, moved to a new industrial unit and then decided to invest in some new ICT. They did it all on the cheap — second-hand computers, cables and wires running everywhere — and within the first week three people had fallen over and hurt themselves at work. There was no clear way of paying anybody; it just came out of the money that had come in during the week. Training was chaos: when one person did not turn up for 3 days, they called him up and sacked him — that was just the start of the problems. He has now taken the business to court; something about discrimination on the grounds of his disability. No one has time to talk to one another, paperwork is everywhere, nothing is filed and no one knows what is going on. It took them nearly 6 days to find out that the website had gone down; they should have realised because orders had stopped coming in, but they were so far behind with the orders that they did not notice. No one really knows how to use the application software that they have had installed on the computers, and there just never seems to be any time to do anything, apart from to make toys.

Fotolia

AO1–AO2 questions

1 The business may have created jobs, but cash flow seems to be a problem. What does this mean?   *(2 marks)*

2 What software should the company use to help sort out paying wages?   *(2 marks)*

3 What is meant by 'disability discrimination'?   *(4 marks)*

4 There seems to be confusion about routine and non-routine tasks. Briefly explain the difference.   *(6 marks)*

5 Which law should they have taken into account before laying wires
   and cables? *(2 marks)*

6 How should the business deal with urgent and non-urgent communication?
   Explain the difference. *(6 marks)*

7 Briefly explain the importance of administration. *(4 marks)*

8 There is no storage and retrieval of information in the business.
   Why is this such a problem? *(4 marks)*

9 Identify THREE key stakeholders in the business. *(3 marks)*

10 There appears to be no structure to the business.
   How might a hierarchy help? *(6 marks)*

AO3 questions

1 The business may have grown, but growth has caused a range
   of problems. What are they and how might this affect the long-term
   success of the business? *(8 marks)*

2 Someone should be responsible for routine and non-routine
   decision making. Who should this be and what do these two types
   of decision making mean? *(8 marks)*

3 Explain why it may have been a bad idea to install second-hand ICT. *(8 marks)*

4 All of the employees are on full-time temporary contracts.
   What does this mean? *(6 marks)*

5 Training has consisted of showing people how to do things and
   then expecting them to get on with it. What type of training is this
   and why do you think it has not been effective? *(8 marks)*

6 The person who has taken the business to court is partially sighted and
   did give one of the owners a letter from the hospital explaining that he
   would be away for a few days after an operation. Why might it be the case
   that the business could be accused of not following equal opportunities? *(6 marks)*

7 Most of the communication that goes on in the business is informal and
   oral. Why might this be a problem? *(6 marks)*

8 How should the business go about making sure that everyone who needs
   to use application software is shown how to use it? *(8 marks)*

9 How can the business ensure that the website, being the source of most
   of its sales, is properly maintained and is running effectively? *(8 marks)*

10 How might understanding the importance of business administration be
   a major way forward for the business? *(8 marks)*

Case study 4

Computer and Data Solution Partners

Three friends finished their degrees in computing at the same time. None of them knew exactly what they wanted to do, so they decided to set up a computer consultancy business. It quickly turned into a repair business. One deals with input devices, another with storage and the third with output devices. This sometimes means that all three of them have to go to the same customer. It is not an ideal situation, as it wastes a great deal of their time, and they want to reorganise how the work should be done. They only have a tiny office and hot desk the one workstation they have, with the remainder of the office full of computer spares. None of them has any experience in management. Everything, apart from the work itself, is carried out by other people for them, including preparing their invoices, doing their accounts, organising their advertising and every other function of the business. They are finding that this is eating up over 60% of what they earn. The three of them decide to sit down and discuss how the business should develop; they all know that radical change is necessary, but none of them seems willing to suggest anything in case the other two disagree. They are happy to take on employees of their own, but they want to retain control of the business and decide how it should develop in the future. All three are keen to continue dealing directly with customers, as they like the challenges it brings.

AO1–AO2 questions

1 Suggest THREE common input devices that the business would need to deal with.   *(3 marks)*

2 Suggest THREE storage devices that the business would need to deal with.   *(3 marks)*

3 Suggest THREE common output devices that the business would need to deal with.   *(3 marks)*

4 Who are the stakeholders of the business?   *(2 marks)*

5 Suggest THREE documents that would have to be prepared if the business were to take on employees.   *(3 marks)*

6 If the three partners could not train someone to do their administration for them, how could the training be delivered?   *(2 marks)*

7 Suggest FOUR areas of potential discrimination that the partners would have to be careful about if they were to take on employees. *(4 marks)*

8 Suggest THREE key job roles that employees could do for the partners. *(3 marks)*

9 What is hot desking? *(2 marks)*

10 The partners are sharing information with others about their customers. Which law do they need to be aware of and careful about? *(2 marks)*

AO3 questions

1 Suggest how appointing a business administrator could greatly assist the running of the business. *(6 marks)*

2 Suggest how the three partners should reorganise the way they handle customer calls. Explain your suggestions. *(8 marks)*

3 Briefly explain how the partners should externally recruit employees. *(6 marks)*

4 Suggest how the partners could reward their new employees and explain the elements of a typical reward package. *(8 marks)*

5 The three partners are very good communicators, but they do not always choose the right way of passing information on to each another. Suggest THREE likely oral and THREE likely written communication media that would be appropriate and explain why. *(9 marks)*

6 The partners have decided to try to attract additional finance for the business to help them expand and take on employees. They want to prepare a professional presentation. Suggest how this could be achieved. *(8 marks)*

7 A friend of theirs has suggested that they should use the internet in order to attract more customers from a wider area, but the partners are not so sure. What might be the downside of offering their services to a broader customer base? *(6 marks)*

8 All three partners work on repairs on a bench. They often have to carry heavy equipment and are all suffering with back problems. What is ergonomics and why is this important? *(6 marks)*

9 One of the areas that they did not cover in their degree course was the potential dangers of working with electrical equipment. Suggest TWO laws that they should be aware of and make FOUR suggestions regarding potential risks or hazards. *(6 marks)*

10 One of the partners has read about multi-skilling. He does not understand precisely what it means. Explain the term and how it could apply to this business. *(8 marks)*

Practice exam

Time allowed: 1 hour

The marks for each question are shown in brackets. The maximum mark for the paper is 60. You will need to use good, clear English. Quality of written communication will be assessed in questions 2(c), 2(e)(ii), 3(e), 4(b) and 4(c).

Total marks for this question: 9 marks

Question 1

Read the scenario, then answer the question that follows.

Scenario

Frankum Miniatures manufactures porcelain and pottery figures for the collectable market. It is a family business, with two generations of the Frankum family owning all of the shares. The company employs two miniatures designers, four people in the casting unit, two warehouse and despatch employees, three people in sales and marketing, and four in accounts and administration. The business has been running for 60 years and has an international market, although the bulk of its sales are in Britain, Europe and the United States.

Frankum Miniatures has decided to invest in a computer network. The business wants to choose a range of ergonomic data input devices. Name the data input devices shown below and explain the benefits of each device to the business.

(9 marks)

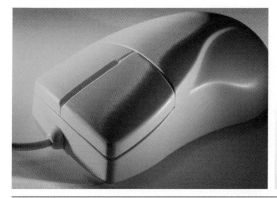 

Total marks for this question: 19 marks

Question 2

Read Item A, then answer the questions that follow.

Item A

Frankum Miniatures has a large office area above the main factory floor. All of the employees are full time. The office is extremely noisy, with people on the telephone and people coming in and out of the offices from the factory floor. At the beginning of each week, Simon Frankum, the managing director, calls a half-hour meeting to announce targets and objectives for the coming week. All staff attend.

(a) **State one business objective that Frankum Miniatures may have identified.**

(1 mark)

(b) **State one group of stakeholders that the business has in addition to the shareholders.**

(1 mark)

(c) **Sandra, the general manager of the office, is keen to reorganise the office space and install cellular offices. Do you think that the business will benefit from this? Explain your answer.**

(5 marks)

(d) **Using an example from the business, explain what is meant by 'internal communication'.**

(2 marks)

(e) **Simon begins the meeting each week by announcing the sales figures for the previous week and how they compare to the targets the business had set itself. There is little time for discussion at the meetings, as they are only half an hour.**

   (i) **Is it a good idea to discuss sales figures with all of the staff? Explain your answer.**

(4 marks)

   (ii) **How could the meetings be better organised to encourage wider contribution of ideas?**

(6 marks)

Total marks for this question: 15 marks

Question 3

Read Item B, then answer the questions that follow.

Item B

Frankum Miniatures has an e-commerce enabled website. It contains numerous photographs and descriptions of the products that it sells. The business relies on a website consultant, who comes in 1 day a week to update or upgrade the website. Simon in particular believes that the website could be far better and have more features.

(a) **Explain TWO advantages of being able to sell products direct to customers.**

(4 marks)

(b) **Clive, one of the designers, would like to put a designer's blog on the website. Explain what is meant by a 'blog'.**

(2 marks)

Read Item C, then answer the questions that follow.

Item C

Most of the office records are still paper-based, particularly those dealing with suppliers and with business customers. Sandra wants to switch over almost completely to computerised records. She knows that this will take some time, but she is sure that it will benefit the business in the longer term.

(c) **Suggest one reason why it might be more efficient to have computerised records.**

(2 marks)

(d) Sandra wants to set up a relational database. What does this mean? *(2 marks)*

(e) How might the accounts department benefit from being able to access the data that it uses electronically rather than from paper records? *(5 marks)*

Total marks for this question: 17 marks

Question 4

Read Item D, then answer the questions that follow.

Item D

A recent meeting of the directors of the company saw a decision being made to take on a new designer. They want to expand the number of products that they produce each month and target new markets abroad. The design work is a technical role, requiring artistic skill and knowledge of casting and design. The business intends to advertise the post in national newspapers and in trade magazines.

(a) Hilary, who has been working as an assistant to the designers for the last 4 years, thinks that she has all of the skills needed to take up the post. If she were given the job, what kind of recruitment would this be and why? *(2 marks)*

(b) If the business were to press ahead with advertising for the post, explain clearly the stages in the recruitment process that would aim to select the best possible candidate. *(10 marks)*

(c) Hilary has been doing her own design work at home and knows exactly how all of the processes work in the factory. Should the business offer her the job and save on the recruitment expenses? Explain your answer. *(5 marks)*

Unit 9
Using ICT in business

What is the unit about?

Unit 9 introduces you to a range of software applications. Businesses use software applications to support their functions and operations. They assist businesses to capture, store, retrieve and analyse data.

Unit 9 is, above all, a practical unit. It has one main section, but it is split into seven separate parts:

- *Selection and use of appropriate software for business purposes.* This explains about using the right kind of software for different data types, processing data, designing ways to present data and how to import objects or data from one application to another.
- *Word processing.* This is about creating documents, using fonts and page layouts, using graphics and combining text with graphics.
- *Spreadsheets.* This explains about creating spreadsheets, manipulating data, creating tables, keying in labels, values, formulae and functions, validation rules, conditional formatting and creating charts.
- *Databases.* This covers designing and creating data capture forms, database tables, sorting, searching and filtering records and creating reports.
- *Graphics.* This part is about creating and editing graphics and combining text with graphics.
- *Presentation software.* This involves creating slides, transitions and animations, modifying presentations and creating presenter notes and handouts.
- *Web authoring.* This explains about creating a business web page, animating text and creating hyperlinks.

Unit 9 is extremely important as it is the link between Unit 8 and Unit 10. In Unit 8 you looked at business functions and communication and the importance of ICT. In Unit 9 you look at the practical use of application software. In Unit 10 you will combine the knowledge from these two units to help you carry out a series of tasks.

What about the exam?

This is a computer-based examination that lasts for 1½ hours. There are 60 marks available and in all, the exam is worth 35% of this GCSE. The exam consists of a number of tasks, usually no more than three. It begins with a case study or scenario. All the questions relate to the case study and you will be asked to carry out a series of tasks based on material that is given to you. You will also be asked questions about particular types of communication, or file or document formats, and be asked your opinion about them. Each set of tasks is worth a number of marks — up to around 20 or so per task. Each of the tasks is also broken down into a number of steps. Unlike Unit 8, you will have to do the tasks in order, as it will be impossible for you to do some of the later tasks without having attempted the earlier ones. Some of these smaller tasks are only worth 2 or so marks. Pay attention to the number of marks that are available, particularly when you are asked to explain things, and always make sure that you save your work and print off hard copies.

How do I get a good grade?

Again there are three assessment objectives (AO1 to AO3), but some of the tasks will also assess the quality of your written work, so it is important to make sure that you have spell-checked and grammar-checked everything that you produce. On the exam paper it tells you which questions are being assessed in this way. It is important to pace yourself in this examination, as there are many things to do and only an hour and a half in which to do them. You have about 1½ minutes for every mark that is available.

Topic 19
Software and data

What the specification requires

You will need to be able to select and then use appropriate software for particular functions. You also need to be aware that data can be in a number of different formats and come from a variety of different sources.

In brief

Businesses need to capture, analyse and **disseminate** a huge variety of different data types. Data can be internally or externally generated, and can be **qualitative** or **quantitative** in nature.

Revision notes

In order to assist business functions or operations and to be able to make decisions, businesses need to capture and store data. It is not just sufficient to store those data; something has to be done with them for the data to be valuable:

- The captured data need to be put into a format, such as a database, so that they can easily be retrieved and looked at.
- Ideally, the data should be easy to analyse. Data records are often called raw data because they are just data that have not been organised in any particular way.
- The data then need to be disseminated, or communicated, to those that need to see the information.
- To make this dissemination effective, the data need to be formatted in different ways, such as charts, tables or graphs.
- Data can come from a variety of different sources; the business itself generates data and there are various external sources of data that can also be valuable, as can be seen in the following table.

Fotolia

Data need to be formatted in different ways to be used effectively

Internal data sources	External data sources
■ Customer records	■ Internet
■ Electronic point of sale (EPOS)	■ Government statistics
■ Monitoring website and website transactions	■ Libraries
■ Accounts records	■ Universities
■ Production information	■ **Company reports**
■ Sales figures	■ Research agencies
■ Customer loyalty schemes	■ Trade magazines, newspapers and journals

There is no point in just collecting data unless the business knows how it is going to use them. The business should use them to make better judgements and decisions, and to keep up-to-date. Some data have to be kept for legal purposes and other data will have to be collected, analysed and formatted so that they can be passed on to stakeholders of the business. Businesses tend to use the Microsoft Office suite to do this, as it provides an integrated set of software applications that can carry out most of the data processing and presentation tasks that might be required. The Microsoft Office suite includes:

- Word — primarily used for text processing, but also used for producing other documents, such as newsletters.
- Excel — designed to process numerical data. Spreadsheets are created and formulae can be added to make calculations.
- Access — effectively an electronic filing system. Templates can be amended or personalised, allowing instant access and the ability to update.
- PowerPoint — presentation software that provides templates that can be amended. This is ideal for live, onscreen presentations, or each slide can be printed off and referred to on paper.

Speak the language

company report — a report that has to be produced by all limited companies, and which details their financial data; it is circulated to all shareholders and is available to any member of the public to read

disseminate — communicating the data to those who need to see or use them

qualitative data — text-based data, such as newspaper articles or reports

quantitative data — numerical or graphical data, either from accounts records or from statistics

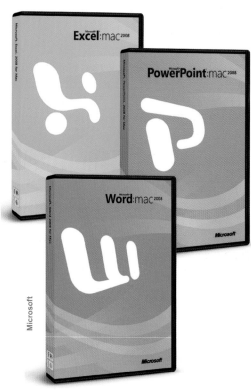

In a nutshell

A business needs to capture, store, retrieve, analyse and disseminate data in the most appropriate format for the individual or group for which the data are being prepared. This means choosing the right software to process those data and then designing a format that suits the purpose. Data can be largely text (qualitative) or numerical and graphical (quantitative). The data can be generated either internally or externally.

Test yourself

Antorkas Food Stores Ltd is a catering wholesaler that supplies Greek and Cypriot restaurants in the London area. It has a basic computer system, but most of its documents are paper-based. This often leads to problems if paperwork is lost. Sometimes orders to customers are wrong and the business has run out of stock of particular items when staff thought there were plenty in the warehouse.

1 The owners of the business want to set up a database to store data regarding their suppliers. Suggest SIX fields that should be included in that database. *(6 marks)*

2 The business wants to try to focus on its top business customers. Which functional areas of Antorkas Food Stores Ltd would be interested in finding out this information? Explain your answer. *(9 marks)*

Boost your grade Each of the different software applications has specific strengths and weaknesses. Using a combination of the applications, businesses are able to transfer data from one application to another. They can then carry out additional data processing and present the data in an easy-to-understand format that can be readily used by individuals.

Topic 20
Uses and presentation of data

What the specification requires

You will need to understand that there are various formats that can be used to present data and that it is possible to **import** and **export** objects or data from one software application to another.

In brief

While it is important to capture, store and retrieve data, it is equally important to make sure that they are presented in the right format. This means choosing not only the right format but also the correct software application to do the job. If the business is using a suite of software applications, it is relatively easy to import and export data from one software application to another.

Revision notes

Even the simplest word-processed document has a particular format, rules or conventions as to how it should look. Application software such as Word has ready-made **templates** for documents, such as a memorandum or a letter. But many businesses choose to personalise the format by amending it. Spreadsheets and databases that can be used both to capture data and to perform calculations need to be **customised**, in order for them to do the job that the business needs them to do. Both of these types of software allow data to be incorporated into a word-processed document, or produce data in the form of tables, graphs or charts. A business can use presentation software or desktop publishing to create eye-catching presentations, newsletters or advertisements. This means using headlines, being as brief as possible and encouraging the reader to make a decision or take action as a result of what they have read.

It is easy to import and export data from one document to another. Pictures, text, graphs, charts and tables can all be copied and then pasted into another document, where they can be reformatted using different fonts or colours. It is also possible to export database files into spreadsheets. A business can also use a database as the data source for a list of names and addresses for a mail-merged letter. Having flexibility in terms of what a business can do with data and how they can be moved around, reformatted and presented in different ways, offers huge benefits. It is important to remember that the same data may need to be formatted in different ways for different purposes.

In a nutshell

By following simple formats and rules, anyone who receives a communication in a particular format will have a better chance of understanding the information that is contained in it. This means that each software application is ideal for different purposes. A word-processing document would not be ideal for the accounts department, which wants to look at a series of figures and make calculations. Businesses use a range of different software applications and it is possible to import or export data from one application to another, so that additional processing and formatting can take place.

Speak the language

customised — refers to a basic template or format for a document that has been amended so that it is personal and specific to the business or to a particular task

export — select data from one software application to import into another software application

import — bring in data from another source or software application

template — a standardised format of a document, spreadsheet or database that has been prepared by the makers of the software application or customised by the business

Test yourself

A business has decided that it wants to put up a simple, one-page job advertisement in local shops and on notice boards and to print 1,000 of them to distribute around the nearest houses to the business premises. The information has to include the job title — night-watchperson — and it should also contain the duties, which are to ensure that the business premises are secure overnight and to be on call if the alarm goes off. No qualifications are required, as all necessary training will be given. The applicant will be given a basic salary and a small additional payment each time they are called out if the alarm goes off. The closing date is the 19th of next month. To apply the candidates must visit the premises in person and collect an application pack. They should hand in a CV at the same time. The job code is 67NWM1.

Task

Design a suitable advertisement containing all of the information above, using a software application of your choice. Print off a hard copy of your advertisement.

(15 marks)

Boost your grade If a business were announcing the launch of a new product or service, it might have to use a number of different formats and software applications to ensure that the news reaches all of its stakeholders. Leaflets and advertisements would be designed for customers, notices or newsletters for employees, letters to suppliers for business customers, and press releases and publicity material for newspapers and magazines. The data contained in the communications would be broadly similar, but in each case the format and design would be different, to match the needs of the audience.

Topic 21
Word processing basics

What the specification requires

You will need to understand what is necessary in order to create a document for a specific business purpose and how to use a range of **fonts** and **page layouts**.

In brief

The text in documents needs to be accurate and error free. Word processing is one of the most commonly used software applications for producing documents. There are many different business documents with specific formats. In order to get the best out of word-processing software, it is important to try to use a range of different formats, including paragraphs, bullet points, alignment, tables and **headers and footers**.

Revision notes

Software applications such as Word allow the user to create either a blank document or any number of different types of document, such as agendas, invoices or letters, from existing templates. Regardless of the type of document being created, it is important to ensure that:

- the copy is accurate and it does not have spelling mistakes or grammatical errors
- the right type of **line spacing** is used
- a suitable alignment — left, right or centred — is used
- capital letters are used as and when required
- text appears either in bold or italics if necessary
- bullet points and numbering are used when appropriate
- complicated data appear in tables
- headers and footers are used if necessary, as well as page numbering

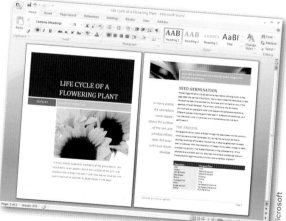

Microsoft

Businesses will send out business letters to individuals or other businesses outside the organisation. There are two documents that are related to meetings:

- *Agendas*. These list all of the topics that will be discussed at the meeting, in the order in which those topics will be discussed.

- *Minutes*. These are accurate written records of the previous meeting and are useful so that individuals can be reminded about what was agreed and whether they were required to do anything as a result of decisions that were made.

Businesses will also use advertisements and flyers to inform potential customers about their products and services, perhaps telling them about special events, offers, changes to opening times or the arrival of new products or services.

In a nutshell

One of the most commonly used software applications is Word, which is essentially a word-processing software package. The software prompts you to amend spelling mistakes or grammatical errors. There are simple shortcut keys to help with line spacing, capitalisation and the use of bold or italics. You can change the look by amending the alignment or indenting lines or paragraphs. Particular points can be highlighted by using bulleted points or numbers, or by inserting tables or text boxes.

Speak the language

font — a particular style of text, such as Arial, Times New Roman or Calibri; the size of the font can be adjusted— normally 11 or 12 point for business use

headers and footers — a header can consist of name, date or other information that will appear at the top of every page of the document; a footer is similar but appears at the bottom of every page and usually includes the page number

line spacing — the gap between each line of the text (e.g. single- or double-line spacing); the lower the number, the smaller the space between each of the lines of text

page layout — the way in which the page will appear, including the number of columns, indentation, spacing, borders, margins and orientation of the paper through the printer

Test yourself

You are busy at work in a sales department and you are passed a letter from a regular customer who is complaining that the last order that they received was incorrect. They had no time to check the order when it arrived and only when they opened the boxes did they discover the problem.

Task

You need to write back and tell them that, although they have signed for the order, a sales representative will visit them on Monday of next week. In the meantime, they should not do anything with the delivered items. Your letter needs to be sent to:

Mr Brian Philpott, 76 Smith Road, Manchester MO4 9BT

The sales representative will be there in the morning. Design your own company headed paper and sign it yourself after you have printed off a hard copy.

(15 marks)

Boost your grade In the examination, pay attention to the instructions in the task. The task will tell you precisely what type of document format is required. In many cases you will be given a blank template for that particular document type; make sure that you use it and do not try to make up your own page format and layout. Make sure, too, that whatever you have typed into a document is accurate; spell-check it and make sure there are no grammatical errors. If you are told to use text features do so; otherwise, do not.

Topic 22
Word processing and graphics

What the specification requires

You will need to be able to use a range of graphics and combine text and graphics.

In brief

A wide variety of graphics can be used to enhance the look of a word-processed document. Some of the graphics are simple pictures, drawings or diagrams. Others allow you to **manipulate text**. You can also **orientate** the text to appear behind, around, above or underneath graphics.

Revision notes

You will need to be able to produce a range of different graphics, including the following:

■ *Callouts*. These are basically like speech bubbles and can be used to feature quotes or phrases. In Word you can access these by choosing the insert tab and then selecting shapes and clicking on the type of callout you prefer. You can then position the callout and type into it and resize it as you need.

■ *WordArt*. This is a great tool to use for headings or for key points that you want to make stand out in the document. WordArt can also be accessed using the insert menu. You will be offered a selection of types of WordArt. It is important not to worry too much about the colour, as this can be changed later. Whatever you type into the WordArt box will appear in that format.

■ *Pictures*. A wide variety of different pictures, drawings and diagrams can be used. Again, all of them are available via the insert menu tab. You can use ClipArt, shapes, SmartArt and charts. If you choose 'picture', the computer will find where they are being stored on the machine and give you the option to choose one of them. You simply insert it into the document then position or resize it as required. SmartArt can be used to make basic diagrams. Shapes can include arrows, flowcharts and lines. Charts allow you to create a basic graph, which is similar to an Excel spreadsheet. You have to type in the data and change the labels to match the data you wish to feature.

- *Borders*. Using the page layout tab, you can choose various options. You can fit the text into a box or a shadow or even see it in 3D. You can also decide on the colour and width or line style you prefer. You can add borders to text, whole pages or just objects that you have inserted.

A good way of getting the best out of the layout of a particular page is to think about how you are going to combine the text and graphics. Pictures do not have to sit on their own with a blank space to their left or right; they can have text flowing around them. By combining text and graphics properly, you can produce a professional-looking document.

Once you have inserted a graphic, you can right click on it. One of the options is known as **text wrapping**. This allows you to position the object in relation to the text.

Speak the language

manipulate text — format or organise the text to improve the way in which it is presented and appears to the reader

orientate — combine text and graphics by deciding how the graphic will appear within the text

text wrapping — fixing the position of the text in relation to the graphic, whatever the shape or size of the graphic

In a nutshell

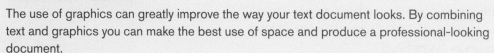

The use of graphics can greatly improve the way your text document looks. By combining text and graphics you can make the best use of space and produce a professional-looking document.

Test yourself

Your boss has asked you to design a very simple notice for a meeting at work. You have been instructed to find a piece of ClipArt that features two people. You should then insert, over the top of the piece of ClipArt, two callouts. The first person should be saying, 'When is the meeting?' and the second one should be replying, 'It is every Monday at 4.30 in the canteen'. Your finished work should be A4 size, landscape and in at least three colours.

(15 marks)

Boost your grade

It is not advisable to make a single text and graphics page too busy, cluttered or confusing. Simply using a single graphic and, perhaps, a callout or a piece of WordArt is far more effective than jumbling up the page with lots of features. Remember to try to draw the reader's attention to the most important part of the page. This is usually the key information, such as a telephone number, address, or how to act once they have read the information. Remember also that if you spend too much time making sure that your document looks attractive, you may not have invested that vital amount of time in ensuring that there are no spelling mistakes or grammatical errors.

Topic 23
Spreadsheet basics

What the specification requires

You will need to be able to input data into a spreadsheet and you will also need to be able to format rows, cells and column widths.

In brief

A spreadsheet is used to process numbers. It can be used to **plot graphs** and **rank data**. Using **formulae**, you can also make calculations. Each spreadsheet document or file is known as a workbook and comprises a number of worksheets. It is possible to format fonts and cells and to change the width of columns for long strings of data.

Revision notes

Spreadsheets are used to process numbers, and businesses regularly use them for budgeting and forecasting financial data. The basic spreadsheet is known as a **workbook**, consisting of a number of worksheets. Each of these worksheets is like a document page, and you can move from one worksheet to another. The worksheets are made up of a grid of columns and rows. You can enter data into any of these cells. Inputting data, including headings and titles, is straightforward; simply click on the cell and then input the data, heading or title. As with a Word document, you can also include headers and footers. You can easily change the font format and choose the font style, size and colour. You can also put in patterns behind the colours or fill the cells with colour. At the top of each column, and at the side of each row, there is a grey band. By clicking on these, you can edit the name of that column or row.

Speak the language

formula — a sum, such as an addition, multiplication, subtraction or division, that instructs the software to make a calculation

plot graphs — input numerical data onto a spreadsheet in order to provide the figures required to create a graph

rank data — sort data numerically, alphabetically or chronologically

workbook — a spreadsheet that consists of a number of worksheets or document pages made up of a series of columns and rows

This is known as amending a label. Simple and complex calculations can be made. To add a series of figures, you highlight the cells and then, from the menu, choose AutoSum. This will automatically add up all the figures in the selected cells and give you a total. The cells can also be formatted so that the numbers appear to the right, left or centre. If you need the column to be wider you click on the line between two cells and pull it, with the left mouse button down, to either widen or narrow that cell or column. Rows can be sorted, numerically, alphabetically or chronologically. You can choose to show the spreadsheet with or without the formulae visible. It is also possible to change the orientation of the spreadsheet from portrait to landscape.

In a nutshell

Departments in a business that deal primarily with figures are most likely to use spreadsheets. They are an ideal way in which to summarise numerical data and then to make a series of calculations. The software will also allow you to create clear tables, charts and graphs from the numerical data that have been input into the spreadsheet. Each spreadsheet is known as a workbook and consists of a number of worksheets. It is possible to manipulate the format of each cell, column or row, and it is also possible to insert headings, titles, labels, headers and footers.

Boost your grade Always think carefully about how you create a spreadsheet. Begin by thinking about the data that you will need to input into that spreadsheet and label your columns and rows. Make sure, when you ask the software to make a calculation for you, that you have highlighted the correct cells. A summary of the formula is visible and make sure that you check it for accuracy. Do not over use colour or background shapes and patterns. The numerical data need to be clear.

Test yourself

A new retail store has just put together the sales figures for its first 10 days of trading. It uses three departmental codes: cards (01), stationery (02) and pens (03). The figures are summarised opposite.

Day	Code 01	Code 02	Code 03
1	£1,000	£1,500	£500
2	£600	£1,700	£450
3	£700	£1,400	£300
4	£900	£1,200	£600
5	£400	£1,600	£700
6	£350	£1,200	£160
7	£380	£1,100	£750
8	£390	£750	£900
9	£500	£900	£950
10	£440	£880	£1,100

Tasks

1 Input the data into a spreadsheet. *(5 marks)*

2 Which was the best and which was the worst day in terms of sales for all departments? *(5 marks)*

3 Which was the worst- and which was the best-performing department over the first 10 days? *(5 marks)*

Topic 24
Spreadsheets, formulae and charts

What the specification requires

You will need to be able to use formulae and functions to carry out a range of calculations. You should also be able to select data series to create charts and use a variety of different formats.

In brief

As you know, a workbook contains a number of worksheets. You can bring these together or **consolidate** them. You can also set up **data validation**, which means that only certain information can go into particular cells. **Conditional formatting** can be used to highlight the most important cells or ranges. For full effect you can also transform the data on a series of worksheets into charts and choose the format of a chart that best suits the circumstances.

Revision notes

It is often necessary to bring together data that have been inputted on to different worksheets within a single workbook. Consolidation can be by:

- position — data from the same cell numbers, rows or columns
- category — data from the same rows or columns if they have the same label
- formula — data that have undergone the same calculation on a different worksheet

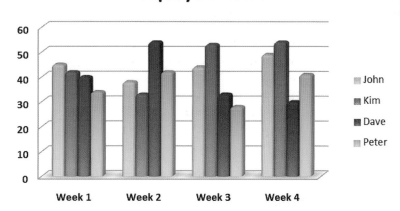

To save time, many businesses set up data validation on their spreadsheets. This means turning cells effectively into drop-down menus. You simply select the item that you wish to use each time. Typically, they might be names, departments, product numbers or item names. It is also possible to use conditional formatting. This allows you to highlight the most important cells or ranges.

Conditional formatting can be:

- two colour — for example, the highest and the lowest
- three colour — for example, the highest, lowest and middle values
- best or worst values
- cells that only contain either text or numbers or dates or times
- cells that contain unique numbers
- cells that contain duplicate values

A useful aspect of spreadsheet software is the ability to transform strings of figures into graphical images. These are known as charts or graphs. Excel has a Chart Wizard, which allows you to choose the type of graph and then to label the *x*- and *y*-axes and give the graph a title. The main choices are:

- line diagrams
- bar charts
- pie charts

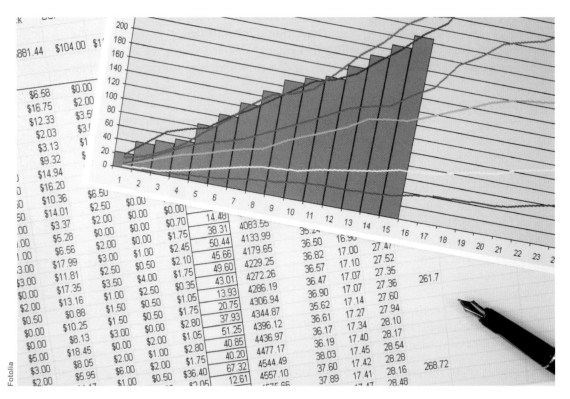

Spreadsheet software can transform figures into graphical images, such as charts or graphs

In a nutshell

As application software, spreadsheets are far more powerful and versatile than simple adding machines. They can perform a wide range of different calculations, and by applying validation rules it is much quicker to input data onto the spreadsheets. Conditional formatting can be used to highlight key figures. In order to get the full effect of the data that have been inputted, they can be transformed into a variety of different charts. This allows key figures, trends and other numerical data to be more obvious to the reader.

Test yourself

A business has been carefully taking note of the sales that it has generated over the past 3 months. There were 12 weeks in this period. The data are shown in the following list, week by week.

£14,500

£16,000

£19,500

£22,000

£12,500

£16,500

£14,250

£19,200

£16,400

£22,000

£15,500

£16,400

Boost your grade Shortcuts to consolidation and data validation are found on the data tab of Excel. From this tab it is also possible to sort, filter and carry out 'what if' analyses, which are often used by businesses to see what might happen in the future if certain events take place. The formula tab offers you a list of different ready-made formulae, which you can apply to particular cells and sets of figures.

Tasks

1 Apply conditional formatting to highlight any weekly sales figures that have fallen below £15,000.

(6 marks)

2 Transform the data into a line graph, adding an appropriate title and data legend.

(9 marks)

Topic 25
Databases

What the specification requires

You will need to understand how to create a **data capture form** and how to create **data input masks**. You will also need to be aware of the fact that there are different **data types**. It is necessary to understand how to insert, edit and delete **fields**.

In brief

When data are being captured, the format into which the data are inputted needs to be logical, as this will form the basis of the database. Data therefore need to be in a particular format, such as text, numbers, or a mixture of the two. If data are collected in a haphazard way, it will be difficult to design a database to suit those data. Without organised collection, some data will be missed and other data will be collected in the wrong format.

Revision notes

Businesses routinely collect data; a customer loyalty card, for example, will hold a customer's name, address and contact details. It will also keep a running total of the amount of money that they have spent and the products and services that they have bought. The data are collected in a logical way and when the business creates a database these data can be inputted into specific fields.

There are a number of different data types:

- text — for names and for simple entries, such as yes or no; this is the default on most database software
- alphanumeric — a combination of letters and numbers, such as an address or postcode
- numeric — numbers only, such as a person's age or telephone number; there is also the option to include numbers to the required decimal place
- dates and times

To control what someone can or cannot put into a field in the database, an input mask can be used. This requires the data to be put into the field in a specific format.

Creating a database is a straightforward task. Software applications such as Access will give you a series of options. All that is necessary is to design the field names and whether or not you want to apply input masks. It is important to remember that you need to save the database before you start inputting data. Each time you add a new record to the database, you type into the blank row at the bottom of the worksheet. The database automatically creates a new blank row. To edit records, use the cursor key to move around. To delete a record, place the cursor in any field of the record row, select edit and then delete record. It is often better to do this in design view. Always make sure that, every time you make a change to your database, you save it.

Speak the language

data capture form — a questionnaire, a series of questions or a straightforward form that aims to collect data in a logical and standardised format

data input mask — a device designed to control what someone can or cannot put into a field in a database

data types — whether the field accepts text, alphanumeric, numeric, dates or time

fields — data items recorded in a database, containing information about one subject of the record

In a nutshell

When designing a data capture sheet, it is important to think about not only what data you want to collect, but also what format you want those data to be in. This means that the creation of the database is far more straightforward, as all of the data will appear in the same order and in the same format. Data records and fields can be inserted, edited or deleted.

Test yourself

1 What data type would be used for a person's name? *(2 marks)*

2 Access has database templates. What do you understand by this statement? *(4 marks)*

3 Why might a customer fill in a warranty card? Suggest what information might be included on it. *(6 marks)*

4 Why might a date of birth require the input of eight numbers and in what format is it likely to appear? *(3 marks)*

Boost your grade

Businesses will routinely collect data in specific formats, when customers fill in warranty cards, or guarantees. They may also collect information from application forms or questionnaires. Libraries collect data in a specific format, with records of all books and other items that an individual has borrowed. Barcode readers are used by businesses to collect information about a specific product. By checking the barcode, they can search the database to see how many of these items are in stock. Each time an item is sold, by scanning the barcode one item is removed from the database.

What the specification requires

You will need to know how to **sort**, **search** and **filter** records, and you will also need to know how to create **database reports**.

In brief

Searching, sorting and selecting records makes it easier to understand specific data. By using a filter, only records that match search criteria will be shown. Microsoft Access allows you to create a report, with labels, headings and graphics, and will display all the fields from a particularly query.

Revision notes

Software applications like Access can allow you to display data in the order in which you want to see them. You may want to see only particular types of customer on a database, so you could choose the field that you want to filter them by. This type of search is known as a query; it means searching through the records and then selecting only those records that match your criteria.

There are four different ways that you can find specific records in a database:
- by physically looking through them, one at a time
- by searching using specified criteria
- by filtering
- by creating a query or a question that allows you to perform customised searches or filters

You can search using single or multiple criteria and the software will give you the option of whether you want a detailed or summary query.

In order for businesses to make sense of the data contained on their databases, they will often use searches and selection to create particular reports. The reports allow you to group and sort information. The report itself is divided up into several different sections:

- report header — a title or a date on the cover page
- page header — at the top of each page
- group header — at the beginning of each new group of records
- detail — each row of the records
- group footer — at the end of each new group of records
- page footer — usually just the page number
- report footer — at the end of the report (may include the report totals or summaries)

Speak the language

database report — a document that allows you to group and sort information in a summarised form and a suitable format for the presentation of the data

filter — eliminate records from the search that are not relevant

search — look through all of the data records to find those that match particular criteria

sort — rearrange records to make it easier to understand the data, for example by putting the records into alphabetical order

In a nutshell

Large databases, full of a great deal of information, can appear daunting and not very useful. It is only when a business applies a search and then selects specific records that the true value of the database becomes clear. A business can look for particular types of record — perhaps customers who have ordered every month, or customers whose payments are outstanding. To make sense of the data, a business will use a query and may filter the records so that the search only includes those that match particular criteria. It can then create a report — in effect, a summary, which only includes the data records that relate to the search itself. It can use this report without having to go through every single record on the database to find the information.

Test yourself

1 How do you sort by more than one column? *(4 marks)*

2 What do you understand by the term 'navigation'? *(2 marks)*

3 What is a query? *(2 marks)*

4 Which view should you choose before printing out a report to see if everything is in the right place and that the report looks professional? *(2 marks)*

5 What do you understand by the term 'filtering'? Give an example of how it might work. *(5 marks)*

Boost your grade

You can make a database report look very professional by opening it in layout view. You can then choose a particular type of report and use the formatting tab to add titles and labels. You can add titles to existing forms or reports and you can also insert dates and times. Logos can be added by clicking on the formatting tab in layout view. Choose the 'insert picture' option and select the logo, graphic or picture of your choice.

Topic 27
Graphics

What the specification requires

You will need to be able to create freehand and **geometric shapes**, and use **shading**, **patterns** and different **line styles**. You will also need to know how to resize and move graphics.

In brief

The use of graphics, shapes, shading, patterns and different line styles can improve the appearance of a document. This is also extremely useful in the creation of documents for special purposes, such as application forms or invoice templates.

Revision notes

Perhaps the most common type of graphic used in documents is ClipArt. Word-processing software will come with a ready-loaded library of ClipArt images, although there are millions available on the internet. These graphics can be dropped into a document, moved around, resized and then positioned so that the text and the graphics work together, with the text flowing around the graphic. There are different types of graphic and the important thing to remember is to choose one that does not blur if it is enlarged.

Software such as Word also has the facility to allow the user to put in different kinds of geometric shapes, such as arrows, stars, banners, callouts and flow chart symbols. It is also possible to insert text boxes, which can be formatted with different kinds of shading and patterns.

Another useful feature is adding lines. These can be formatted in a host of different ways in terms of the thickness of the line, its colour and whether or not it is solid or a series of dots or dashes. In the AutoShapes menu of Word, there is a line option. This allows you to choose thin or thick lines, lines with dots or dashes, or special lines that can be made up of stars, and gives you the ability to change the colour and select an arrow at each end or just at one end of the line.

It is also important to understand exactly how to deal with graphics inside a document. By clicking on a graphic, a frame will appear around it. The blocks in the corners and halfway along each edge can be used to resize the graphic. By placing the cursor over the graphic it will turn into a black cross and this means you can drag the graphic to a new position within the document.

geometric shapes — for example, arrows, flow chart symbols, callouts, triangles, circles, boxes and stars

line styles — the various options available when choosing a line, referring to its thickness, whether or not it is unbroken or has an arrowhead, and the colour chosen

patterns — these also apply to text boxes or geometric shapes and refer to the background of the box

shading — this determines how a geometric shape, such as a text box, appears, particularly the area around that text box

In a nutshell

If used correctly, graphics, ClipArt, geometric shapes and lines can all improve the appearance of a document. Graphics and geometric shapes can be moved and resized, so that they fit exactly into a position in the document and can also have text flowing around them to produce a professional look. There are millions of graphics available and thousands of different geometric shapes. There are also hundreds of different line styles. By carefully combining these features with the text, the document can be greatly improved, providing they are not over-used or badly positioned.

Test yourself

1 What is meant by the term 'caption'? *(2 marks)*

2 How might you use a text box? *(4 marks)*

3 What would happen if you right-clicked and selected 'cut' over a graphic? *(2 marks)*

4 What type of graphic might you use in order to indicate that part of a form has been designed to be filled in and then clipped out and returned? *(2 marks)*

5 What needs to appear on a graphic in order for you simply to move it? *(1 mark)*

6 What are the TWO basic options when resizing a graphic and what direction would your cursor need to move for each? *(4 marks)*

Boost your grade

Making the text flow around graphics can produce a far more professional look. In the draw menu in Word, select 'text wrapping'. This offers you different choices of how the text will appear around the graphic.
Also pay attention to the alignment of the text.
You can set it so that the graphic appears on the left or right-hand margin, with the text running alongside the graphic. You can also set the alignment so that the graphic appears underneath the text, but make sure that the text is still legible.

Topic 28
Presentation software

What the specification requires

You will need to be able to create slides for a short business presentation and also to create **transitions** and **animations**.

In brief

Software applications such as Microsoft PowerPoint can create professional-looking presentations, either from scratch or by using wizards. Each slide can consist of a mixture of text and graphics and any text or objects on that slide can be animated, so that the user can control the flow of information. Transitions are animations that take place as you move from one slide to the next.

Revision notes

PowerPoint is probably the most commonly used presentation application software. It already has a number of themes and slide styles that you can use. It also has the advantage of allowing you to change colours, fonts and effects. When PowerPoint opens, the application creates a simple opening slide for the presentation. All that is now required is for you to choose a design theme. This can be achieved by clicking on the design tab and looking through the design themes. Each different slide can have a different look. The options are:

- title
- title and content
- section header
- two content
- comparison
- title only
- content with caption
- picture with caption

To insert text, you click on a text box object and type into it. The text boxes can be resized, as can the text within them. You can also use bullet points and numbering within the textbox.

It is possible to animate text and objects. You can apply animation effects by clicking on the animations tab in the animations group. Simply select 'fade', 'wipe' or 'fly in' and the program will then show you the effect. Animation on a slide helps to provide more of a visual interest to the presentation. You can also animate the whole presentation, so that once you have started it up it will run, using all of the slide-based animations.

Transitions can be created by using the animation tab too. The transitions option will give you a number of choices, including:

- fades and dissolves
- wipes
- push and cover
- stripes and bars
- random

Speak the language

animation — an on-slide effect, which allows text or objects to appear in a specified order and in a particular way

transition — when one slide is replaced by another during the presentation

You can assign sounds to each of these transitions. It is also possible to set the speed at which the transitions take place, so that you can time the overall length of the presentation.

In a nutshell

A business will use PowerPoint to create presentations and will utilise animations and transitions to keep the audience focused and interested. Presentations should only feature key phrases; the slides should be easy to follow. Fancy fonts should be avoided and care should be given when choosing contrasting colours. Slide design should be as straightforward as possible. If transitions and animations are too complicated, the audience could become distracted.

Boost your grade

Most presentations are unsatisfactory, as they are boring or have been over-animated. Ensure that you only use animations when they are absolutely necessary and for effect. Although multiple animations will show that you know how to use the software, it will be very difficult for the audience to follow the presentation. Always bear in mind that graphs, charts and photographs can add interest to the presentation. Try to avoid having text-only slides. Always keep your presentation down to a minimum number of slides; around one slide per minute for a presentation is about right. Never over-use capital letters, as they are more difficult to read. Make sure that the most important information is at the top of the slide. Never have more than three numbered or bulleted points per slide; the more clear space on each slide, the easier it will be to read. Try not to overdo the colour, but stick to a colour theme throughout the presentation.

Test yourself

1 How might text in a Word document be useful when creating a presentation? Explain your answer. *(6 marks)*

2 How might the information contained in an Excel spreadsheet be used in a presentation? Explain your answer. *(6 marks)*

3 Suggest THREE benefits of animation. *(3 marks)*

Topic 29
Presentation software and notes

What the specification requires

You will need to be able to modify presentations and to create **presenter notes** and **handouts**.

In brief

To modify a presentation, you will need to be able to resize, **crop**, align and move objects. You might also need to change the background colour, or even add additional slides. It is useful to create presenter notes and handouts to give to the audience.

Revision notes

By right-clicking on an object, a dialogue box will appear. This allows you to change the size and position of that object. You can easily adjust the size of the object by using the arrow keys that are alongside the height and the width. This makes the object either larger or smaller. It is important to remember that, if you change the height, the program will automatically adjust the width so that it stays in proportion.

You can also crop an object, from the left, right, top or bottom. This gives you the extra flexibility to resize the object so that it fits into the space available on the slide. Aligning and moving objects on a slide could not be more straightforward. If you right click on a text box, you can choose left, right, centre or justify from the paragraph group. The easiest way to move an object around is to click on it and the cursor will change into an arrow with a cross. If you keep your left mouse button down, you can move the object around. When you are happy with its new position, you release the left mouse button and the object will be moved to its new position.

The background colour of slides can also be changed easily by clicking on the text box and selecting 'format shape'. From here you can choose:
- background colour
- shadow
- line style
- 3D effects

When you click on a picture and choose 'format', you can re-colour it from a palette of different colours.

On some occasions, you may want to add or insert slides into an existing presentation. You can use existing templates, or even duplicate slides that you have already created. You can, of course, reposition the slide so that it appears at any point in your presentation.

Sometimes it is useful to create a set of presenter notes. This is a rather like having a script, with additional information, so that as the presenter is talking while a particular slide is being viewed, they can make comments and draw the audience's attention to certain issues.

Speak the language

crop — make the shape and size of an object precisely fit the space that you have available for it on a slide

handouts — copies of the slides used in the presentation, with or without room alongside for the audience to take notes

presenter notes — these can be added to a presentation, but made visible only to the presenter, so they can refer to them during the presentation

It is also valuable on some occasions to print the slides as handouts. PowerPoint, for example, offers you the opportunity to print a number of slides on a sheet of A4 or to print fewer slides and leave room for the audience to make notes alongside each slide.

In a nutshell

It is often the case that once a presentation has been created, some changes to it may be required, to improve either the content or the way a particular slide looks. Objects such as graphics and textboxes can be resized. They can also be moved around. If you are unhappy with the colours on a particular slide you can change the background. Once you have looked through the presentation, you may notice something missing, so you can add additional slides and then put them in the order in which you want them to appear. Presenter notes are a useful prompt, as they remind the presenter about key points. Sometimes audiences could benefit from handouts. You can either give them a set of the slides in miniature, or leave space alongside printouts of each slide for them to make their own notes.

Test yourself

1 What is meant by a 'slide library'? Give an example. *(4 marks)*

2 When creating presenter notes, what is a 'notes master'? *(6 marks)*

3 Explain why handouts might be useful for the audience. *(5 marks)*

Boost your grade Make sure that you only have one click per slide. Always use large fonts; never use dark fonts on a dark background. Avoid using annoying animations and silly ClipArt. Never assume that your presentation will work on a different computer; always check first.

What the specification requires

You will need to know how to create a web page and how to compose and input information accurately.

In brief

Software applications such as Microsoft Publisher and Microsoft Word provide basic templates to create web pages. Web pages should have a consistent format. They should be easy to navigate and use **hyperlinks**, **bookmarks** and **navigation bars**, so that users can easily move around the website.

Revision notes

Businesses now reguarly create web pages, as it has become almost essential that they have some kind of presence on the internet. Some websites simply contain basic information about a business's products and services, along with their contact details. Other websites are more sophisticated and allow customers to make online purchases.

Starting a web page in Microsoft Publisher is very similar to working in Word. Websites are just one of the many templates available. The websites tend to fall into three categories:

- classic designs — usually white with splashes of colour
- blank designs — which are somewhat old-fashioned but can easily be modified
- newer designs — some of which will be available as templates, while others may have to be downloaded from the Microsoft website

As with any kind of document, it is important to establish a consistent format. This means that each web page should look broadly the same, with the same background colours, and hyperlinks and navigation bars in the same position, so that they can be easily found.

Each web page consists of a number of text boxes, as with PowerPoint. These are of limited size. You can also reposition the text boxes, swap the existing graphics for new ones and rearrange the page to suit your purpose. You can also import text directly from Word; graphs, charts and tables from Excel; or ClipArt from the internet.

In order to get a consistent format, try to make sure that you do not use too many different types of font, and the paragraphs, line spacing and alignment of text should all be consistent. It is possible to use bullet points and numbered lists. It is important to:

- check spelling
- make sure the grammar is correct
- use different font sizes to emphasise points
- use colour, style and different font types
- make sure your paragraph formats are consistent, including line spacing and indentation

Speak the language

bookmarks — allow the user to store the location of a web page so that they can visit this website again simply by clicking on the bookmark, rather than typing in the URL

hyperlinks — a way of cross-referencing web pages so that by clicking on text or graphics the user can be taken to a new location

navigation bars — also known as link bars, these enable the user with one click to move to a different page of the website

In a nutshell

Even a basic web page gives a business a presence on the internet. It allows the business to set up a contact page, where potential customers can e-mail it. Web pages need to be consistent, uncluttered and professional looking, with a clear design running through all of the pages. They should be easy to navigate, and visitors to the website should be able to find the information they are looking for with the minimum number of clicks.

Test yourself

1 Microsoft Publisher has what is known as a 'content library'. What is the purpose of this and what might you find in it? *(6 marks)*

2 If a customer contacts a business enquiring about its products or services, how could the business use its e-mail address? Suggest FOUR possible uses. *(4 marks)*

3 Why is it not advisable to have a very dark background on a website? Explain your answer. *(5 marks)*

Boost your grade

Just having a website is not sufficient. Potential visitors to the website need to be able to find it. It is therefore important to put key words and phrases on the opening page of the website. When someone types that key word into a search engine, the website will then come up as one of the search results. To get on to the first page of a search engine's results can often cost a great deal of money. Businesses use websites so that they can have a global visibility. They can be open for orders all day every day. If customers can see what products and services are on sale, even if they cannot buy online, it could prompt them to contact the business and make an order.

Topic 31
Web authoring, animation and hyperlinks

What the specification requires

You will need to be able to animate text, change the background colour, use borders and lines, insert images and use **frames**. You will also have to create hyperlinks to enable easier navigation around the website.

In brief

To ensure that your website does not look the same as thousands of others, it is important to be able to **customise** certain features so that the pages are more attractive to visitors. It is also important that users can navigate their way around the website with ease.

Revision notes

You can insert animated text or pictures by simply clicking on 'insert' and then finding that image. If you copy and paste the file, however, it may lose its animated properties.

There are two ways to change the background colour:
- You can use the format tab and choose one of the sets of colour schemes, or devise your own.
- You can change the background by applying one of the existing colour schemes. Each of these can be adjusted, giving you a wide range of variation.

You can use borders and lines to highlight particular parts of a web page. Several different line options are available and you can also determine the colour of that line. Border art is also another option; you can apply any of these and create your own customised borders using pictures and ClipArt.

Images can be inserted via the design gallery. These include:
- accent boxes
- buttons
- navigation bars
- advertisements
- logos

By clicking on the 'picture' option, you can insert ClipArt or images. This gives you access to flow charts, callouts and WordArt. You can also insert objects, such as charts from Excel, a PowerPoint slide or a whole Word document. It is also possible to import video clips and sounds.

A frame is an area on a web page that you have set aside to insert a picture. Perhaps you have not yet found the ideal picture. This simply reserves that space for the picture, which can be inserted at a later date. You can adjust its size and shape, and rotate the frame if you need to.

To enable users to move around the website with the minimum number of clicks, you can insert hyperlinks. These automatically move the user to a new page on the website, or indeed to another website, by clicking on a word or an object such as a picture, which has been given this attribute. An ideal example is to open up an e-mail box if the user clicks 'contact us'. Hyperlinks are easy to create, by either highlighting the text or clicking on an object. Right-click and one of the options is to create a hyperlink. You will, of course, have to insert the destination of the hyperlink.

In a nutshell

With millions of websites for users to visit, a business will always look for a different way of presenting its information and making the website as user-friendly as possible. It will achieve this with a combination of animations, colours, formats, styles, internal and external hyperlinks and, of course, constantly changing content, which is as up-to-date as possible.

Test yourself

1 Why might a website have an advertisement for another company's website and a hyperlink to take the customer to it? *(6 marks)*

2 Where would be the ideal place to send a user if they clicked on 'contact us'? *(2 marks)*

3 In Microsoft Publisher, what do you understand by the term 'accent colour'? *(3 marks)*

4 In Publisher, what are the FOUR options offered in the hyperlink dialogue box? *(4 marks)*

Boost your grade Internal and external hyperlinks are used by most websites. Some websites are complex and have hundreds or thousands of separate pages. A website such as Amazon needs to be able to get the customer to the right page as quickly as possible to encourage them to buy. Websites may also have external links, which could take them to an independent website which has, perhaps, reviewed their products or services. Other businesses have several different websites and the hyperlinks may take the customer to the website that deals with those particular products and services that they are interested in buying.

Section tests

Street Party

In 2 months' time it will be the 200th anniversary of the building of most of the houses along Bradwell Street. The local people wish to celebrate by organising a street party. They are looking for volunteers to cook food, provide tables and chairs, decorate the street and attend a series of meetings over the next few weeks in the run-up to the event.

You have been asked to create a suitable flyer, which can be put through every letterbox in the street. It needs to:

- include a suitable headline, with the date and time of the event
- say why the event is to take place
- ask for volunteers and also announce the first meeting, which will take place in one week's time, at the main coordinator's house, at no. 47
- have suitable graphics or images, and be attractive and easy to read

You should restrict the number of words used so that those who are visually impaired can read the flyer.

Use a suitable piece of application software, employing a variety of fonts, images, colours and layout, to produce an A4 flyer. Print off a copy of your flyer.

Fotolia

Street Party support

At the first meeting it was decided to try to ask the local council to see if it would be interested in helping organise the event and providing some funds. As the secretary of the coordinating committee, you have been asked to write a letter to your local council. You need to:

- include details about the event
- explain why it is being held
- ask whether the council will help you with publicity and give you contact details of the local press and media
- ask if it is prepared to make a small donation to the event
- warn the council that the street may need cleaning after the event has taken place
- ask if it will be necessary to have council staff and/or police on hand for the event

You should write your letter to: Councillor Willis, The Town Hall, High Street, Fenbury FE4 4NN

Street Party database

Fifteen people have offered either to cook or to provide furniture, and some have offered to make decorations. You now need to create a database so that you can search through the records and then contact each group in turn to coordinate their efforts. Use the data from the following table.

Name	House number	Task offered
Mrs Agathokleous	22	Cook
Mr Briggs	14	Furniture
Mrs Jackman	11	Decorations
Mr Taylor	5	Decorations
Mr Lynch	19	Cook
Mr Hall	20	Furniture
Mr Teppit	3	Furniture
Mrs Weatherburn	15	Cook
Mr Watkins	18	Cook
Miss Newland	7	Cook
Mrs Burywood	9	Cook
Mrs Allen	10	Decorations
Mrs Forbes	17	Furniture
Mr Chung	4	Decorations
Mr Jackson	13	Furniture

Create a suitable database for the data in the table and then carry out the following:

- Sort your database into alphabetical order of surname.
- Select only those who offered to cook.
- Print off the names and house numbers of those who have offered to cook using a report format.

Street Party costs

The committee has been trying to work out exactly how much the street party will cost. You know that 160 people have completed forms saying that they will be attending the event. You have estimated that the food will cost £450, decorations an additional £200, street entertainment, including jugglers and a band, will cost £300. The council is insisting that a £150 contribution is made to street cleaning, but it has made a donation of £75. Other costs, including printing of forms, production of flyers etc., has cost another £100. You also estimate that to provide drinks for 160 people will cost £320.

Your task is to create a spreadsheet that totals all of these costs and then you must calculate how much to charge each person who has promised to attend, in order to cover the costs and provide £100 for a donation to a local charity.

Street Party presentation

Happy with your costings and arrangements so far, the committee has now organised a brief presentation that will be made to the local media. You must prepare a short presentation of no more than FIVE slides, detailing the event and all the organisation that has happened so far. You may use any graphics, images, charts or tables that you have already generated in order to complete this task. Your presentation should be timed to last no more than 5 minutes. You should also prepare presenter notes and handouts for the audience.

Street Party web page

The committee has just realised that, over the course of the last 200 years, many hundreds of families have moved into and out of the street. The committee thinks it would be a great idea to try to tell as many ex-residents as possible that the 200-year anniversary street party is taking place. It wants to design a simple two-page website with details about the street party plan and also to provide contact details for ex-residents to get in touch with committee members about attending. Use any material that you have already generated for previous tasks and include the following contact details:

Mrs Sylvia O'Donoghue, 20 Bradwell Street, Fenbury FE4 7AH, e-mail address: Sylvie@totumnet.com

Your main headline should attract the attention of all former residents of Bradwell Street. The media has promised to publicise your website, so you should expect a number of people to visit the site at www.bradwellstreetparty.org

Practice exam

Time allowed: 1 hour 30 minutes

You will need: appropriate computer hardware and software, a stationery folder and 14 sheets of A4 paper

Instructions

In the actual examination, some templates, graphics and text will be provided. For this practice exam, you can generate all of this yourself or use the materials provided online at www.hodderplus.co.uk/philipallan.

You are to attempt all THREE tasks. The paper consists of the following:

Task 1 — Flyer   *(24 marks)*

Task 2 — Database   *(16 marks)*

Task 3 — Presentation   *(20 marks)*

Task 1 — Flyer

Waterslade Floorings has just signed a contract with an American manufacturer to import a revolutionary new non-slip flooring. It is ideal for kitchens, bathrooms and offices. Even if water is on the flooring, it is guaranteed to be non-slip, so it should be ideal also for those with disabilities and the elderly. The business wants to produce a flyer offering the product at a special discounted rate for the first 100 customers. The flooring is £15.99 per metre, including fitting. It is available in 25 different colours and textures and is guaranteed for 10 years. The business's address is 47 The Precinct, Felton, West Midlands BR2 4DT. The telephone number is 0123 45678.

(a) **Select a suitable software application and use a range of tools to create an A4 flyer that will encourage customers to contact the business and book an onsite visit from one of its sales representatives. You should only use two pieces of ClipArt or graphics on your flyer.** *(6 marks)*

Save your flyer as flyer1 and print out a copy.

(b) **The owner of the business would like to know how the flyer was designed. Using Microsoft Word, write a brief explanation to John MacIntosh, the managing director, as an e-mail explaining the reasons for the design of your flyer.** *(8 marks)*

Save your e-mail as email1 and print out a copy.

(c) **Reopen your flyer1 file. John MacIntosh wants to use the flyer as the basis for an advertisement in the local press. Waterslade Floorings has already received a positive response from a number of customers.**

(i) **Make THREE changes to the appearance of your flyer.** *(3 marks)*

Save your file as flyer2 and print out a copy.

(ii) **Label the flyer using callout boxes to show the changes you have made and why you have changed the appearance.** *(7 marks)*

Save your file as flyer3 and print out a copy.

Task 2 — Database

Up until this point the business has not kept a database of its customers, but starting with this new product it wants to do this so that it has the following details:

- customer name and address
- amount of square metres of flooring ordered and total price paid
- how the customer paid
- code number of flooring purchased
- guarantee expiry date

The following people have purchased the new flooring so far:

Mr J. Marx, 47 New Road, West Bromwich	12 sqm £191.88	Debit card	012	2020
Mrs P. Butcher, 12 Caledonian Way, West Bromwich	20 sqm £319.80	Credit card	014	2019
Mr L. Raggesh, 11 The Close, Walsall	40 sqm £639.60	Cash	012	2020
Ms P. Higgins, 12 Blackbird Close, Walsall	10 sqm £159.99	Cheque	017	2020
Mr M. McDonald, The Old Manse, West Bromwich	50 sqm £799.50	Debit card	015	2020
Ms M. Sergiou, 49 Clarence Street, Birmingham	15 sqm £239.85	Credit card	017	2019
Mr P. Thomas, 11 The Street, Birmingham	35 sqm £559.65	Cash	017	2020
Mr A. Buchan, 511 Walsall Road, Birmingham	40 sqm £639.60	Credit card	015	2020

Create the database using suitable fields.

(a) Add to the database Mr B. Gardener of 238 Buckingham Road, Walsall, who purchased 15 sqm of number 011. The price has not been calculated. *(2 marks)*

(b) Search the database to find all customers who have ordered code number 017. *(2 marks)*

(c) Sort these customers by the customer surname into alphabetical order. *(2 marks)*

Print this file in list format.

(d) The business wants to know how the database could be used in the future. It thinks that other fields could be added to make the database more valuable. Add FOUR fields to your database that could contain useful information for the business. *(2 marks)*

Save your edited file and print it in list format showing your new field headings.

(e) Using Word, create an e-mail in response to the following e-mail from the managing director. *(8 marks)*

> Thanks for all the work you've done on the database. I want to contact customers who purchased different code numbers of flooring, as I want to ask them whether they would be happy for us to come round and take photographs for our new brochure. Can you answer the following questions for me?
> ● How do I ensure that I only send one letter out per code, preferably to the person who spent the most?
> ● Do you think this is a good way for us to contact them?

Save your e-mail as e-mail2 and print out a copy.

Task 3 — Presentation

The managing director has decided to try to focus on the many hundreds of takeaways and restaurants in the area and aims to have a major sales push. He has contacted local business groups and asked whether they would be happy for him to make a short presentation, as he believes there are health and safety benefits to the new flooring for businesses. He wants you to create a presentation, which incorporates the following information:

■ special business price of £13.99 per square metre
■ all the codes are available
■ guaranteed fitting within 10 days
■ 60 days to pay
■ hygienic, safe and anti-slip
■ 10-year guarantee
■ free callout for maintenance
■ no fitting fee

(a) Open a suitable software application and create FIVE slides containing the details above and any other information you think might be relevant. You can have transitions and animations.

Save your presentation file as business1. Print all your slides as handouts.

(10 marks)

(b) The managing director has never used presentation software before. He has two key questions.
  (i) Give him ONE advantage and ONE disadvantage of using an electronic presentation instead of a paper one. *(4 marks)*
  (ii) Do you have any tips for the managing director as to timing and how the presentation should be managed? Explain your answers. *(6 marks)*

Save your notes as presentation1 and print out a copy.

Unit 10
Investigating ICT in business

Controlled assessment

Unit 10: Investigating ICT in business is known as a 'controlled assessment' unit. The examination board will set the tasks and when you are supposed to do them. It will also determine how the work that you produce is to be marked.

You will have heard about coursework. In reality, a controlled assessment is not that much different. The biggest difference is that you will be working on a series of tasks that will include some research, under supervised conditions. You will also have a limited amount of time to do the tasks. There is no new content to remember or skills to acquire; everything that you have done in Unit 8 and Unit 9 could be covered in the Unit 10 controlled assessment.

What happens in a controlled assessment?

Well before you have to do your controlled assessment, the examination board will release the background information for the tasks that it will be expecting you to complete. This will be a brief scenario, which sets the scene for the tasks. If you read through this very carefully with your teacher or tutor, you should get a good idea of what is to come. There will be a series of research and investigation tasks. These will make it very clear what is expected of you. There will also be a section that tells you exactly what you have to include in your final presentation.

How to handle the controlled assessment

We already know that you will have to carry out some kind of research or investigation. You will have to sort out the information that you have collected and then use it in some way for your final presentation. You should expect to have to show that you are able to use a range of different application softwares. The research task will probably relate to Unit 8 in some way,

and the skills that you have picked up in Unit 9 will allow you to use the application softwares to the best effect.

When you start your research, it is acceptable to work as a group, but you will not be able to submit group work; it has to be individual work, so make sure that whatever research and information you have collected, you each have a copy of it. The final presentation part is likely to last for between 3 and 4 hours. It might be in one block of time or split up into two or three sessions; it will depend on your school or college.

You need to make sure that anything that you have worked on and anything that you might need is safe. Your teacher or tutor will collect in any work that you have done, but anything else you need must be at hand, as you may need to refer to it later.

Another important thing to remember is that you need to check your spelling, punctuation and grammar. You will get marks for the content of your work, so concentrate on that and do not spend all of your time trying to make your work look pretty. Good layout and design is important, but it will only get you some of the marks.

How to prepare and how to research and investigate

Preparing

You will probably see the controlled assessment at the beginning of the spring term. You will not be able to tackle it until you have completed Unit 8 and Unit 9 because you will not have the knowledge or the skills to attempt it. Remember that there are three assessment objectives (AOs).

If you provide a basic answer and simply describe something and show that you understand it, you will only show that you can recall, select and communicate information; this is AO1. For this assessment objective, you can get a maximum of 12 marks. If you can apply your knowledge and understanding and show that you can plan and carry out tasks and investigations, you can achieve AO2. This can be worth up to 26 marks. To hit the top marks you will need to go for AO3. This means that you will have to analyse, evaluate and justify what you have done. If you reach this level, up to 40 marks are available.

Research and investigation

You will have between 5 and 8 hours to pull together as much information as you possibly can to help you with the tasks. If you overwhelm yourself with information at this point and have not sorted through it and selected only the bits that you need, then you will get in a muddle when it comes to doing the tasks. Make sure anything that you keep is relevant.

Remember that the knowledge and skills you acquired in Unit 8 and Unit 9 will enable you to tackle Unit 10

Any assistance given to you by your teacher or tutor will have to be recorded. To speed up research, work as a group and split up the jobs, but then make sure that everyone has copies of whatever anyone has collected. You should set aside a little time at the end of this process to sort through what has been collected and to discard what you think is irrelevant.

Watch out for command words in the tasks. If the word 'conduct' is used, this means you may need to carry out some research, or a study to find something out. If the word 'develop' is used, you need to build on an idea or a description, perhaps noting advantages and disadvantages. If the word 'identify' is used, that means you have to suggest some way of doing something — perhaps the ideal way. 'Calculate' means literally to perform a sum, such as adding up costs. 'Estimate' means making a guess based on facts and figures. Your personal view can certainly be included in the last one.

Each of the tasks is a practical activity. They are either based on Unit 8, in which case they might be 'identify' or 'calculate'. Alternatively, they will be based on Unit 9, which could mean 'develop' or 'estimate'. In the second case it might be a good plan to use Excel.

Remember that the controlled assessment is actually fairer than coursework. Everyone will have access to the same resources and will have the same amount of time. You will be supervised throughout and everyone will know that the work you produce is your work.

The presentation

Using your time wisely

Hopefully during the research and planning stage of the controlled assessment you will have collected enough information. Part of that also means understanding what you have got and organising it. If you have been sufficiently well organised, you will have had a chance to produce a rough draft of your final presentation already. These last 3 or so hours should be spent making sure that absolutely everything is correct and that you have answered every one of the tasks and questions as fully as you possibly can.

You will not be able to take anything away with you during the final presentation session or sessions. It will be collected in. Also your teachers and tutors will not be able to give you any feedback or help during this final presentation stage. If you have got to this final stage and you still do not understand something, it is too late.

You will be expected to work alone. The final presentation is under examination conditions, but you will be able to use computers, printers and any other equipment or materials that your school or college has prepared.

What is the examiner looking for?

Any exam is a test of your knowledge and skills, but also your time management, decision-making and problem-solving abilities. The examiner wants to see how you have used the information that you have collected and, as we will see, they are also interested in how you analyse and evaluate what you have done.

You must make sure that, if you have been asked to produce screen prints, printouts or any other physical material, you have done this before the end of the 3 hours. If anything is missing, that is your fault and the examiner cannot be expected to hunt for it on your user area on the computer network. Check through the tasks and make sure you have evidence that you have done the task and it is in the format in which you have been asked to present it.

Make sure that you use business and ICT concepts, words or jargon. Do not just drop them into sentences, as the examiner will spot that you do not actually understand what they mean but think you should include them. Make a double check that everything is spelled correctly and that your punctuation and grammar are as accurate as possible. Structure your work and use headings, bullet points and page numbering if these are relevant.

Do not forget that if you have been asked to produce an e-mail and you submit a business letter, you will be penalised because you have not followed the instructions. This is regardless of what might be in that letter.

We will see in the next section that evaluation is very important. This means analysing and evaluating what you have done, so you need to put time aside to complete this part of the tasks. All it means is explaining why you have done something in a particular way, or why you consider one thing to be more important than another.

Evaluation and the marks

What is evaluation?

It is possible for you to pass this GCSE and get a reasonable grade just by doing the tasks and showing that you fully understand business and ICT concepts, and that you have ICT skills and can follow instructions. To unlock better grades you need to evaluate. This means showing that you understand the relative importance of things. You will have a set of findings from your investigation, but not all of those findings are of equal importance; some are more relevant or crucial than others. Evaluating means identifying them and saying why you have identified them. Anyone can list a set of advantages and disadvantages. Evaluating means picking out the most important ones and saying why they are so vital.

Your findings might also suggest a particular way forward, or a way of solving a problem or dealing with an issue. It is also evaluation if you make that suggestion.

There are five levels to AO3. In brief these are:
- Level 0 — you have not made any conclusions, nor have you analysed or evaluated.
- Level 1 — you have conclusions but you have not really explained them.
- Level 2 — you have simple conclusions but your evaluation does not highlight the significant points.
- Level 3 — you have good conclusions and have made a judgement about your findings.
- Level 4 — you have a good range of conclusions and you have evaluated and justified each for its significance.

How does the marking work?

Your teachers and tutors will be the first to mark your controlled assessment, but they will have to follow a mark scheme produced by the examination board. They will have to mark you fairly because the examination board will randomly check their marking.

There are 40 marks available for Unit 10. If you have just done the basic work, you will only get 30% of the marks available to you, so do not expect anything more than an F for Unit 10. If you have reached AO2 standard, which means that you have applied your knowledge and understanding, you are moving towards a C grade for this unit. As we have seen, you need to analyse and evaluate to reach AO3 and only when you do this is it possible to get a B grade or better.

The examination board will produce a checklist as part of its mark scheme. This will include:
- any business or ICT terms that the exam board expects you to include
- acceptable and unacceptable ways to have carried out the research
- the correct formulae to use when making calculations
- the issues that it might expect you to highlight in your conclusions, analysis and evaluation

Practice controlled assessment

Research task

You have been asked to carry out an investigation of websites that review villages, towns and cities. The idea is to create a series of websites that will feature the best and worst aspects of villages, towns and cities around Britain. Your investigation will have two parts.

Part One

Find at least THREE websites that feature information, events, news, history and other information about your local village, town or city. Identify the features (content and layout) that make the website effective in communicating with its users. You should pay particular attention to the website's home page. As part of your findings, you should produce a screen print of the website's home page, and write a report identifying those features of the website that are effective, and those features that could be improved.

Part Two

You need to design a web page that will be called 'yourplacegoodorbad.com'. Replace the 'yourplace' with the name of your village, town or city and include the following information:

- yourplacegoodorbad.com is the site to go to find out the best and worst
- written by locals, for locals and visitors alike
- everything revealed
- best and worst shops
- places to avoid
- food you should not eat
- rip-off attractions
- places to go for free
- fully independent and unbiased

Once you have completed your web page, produce a screen print and a justification of why you have designed your web page in the way you have chosen.

Pointers for this practice assessment

Part One

Where you start to look will be very dependent on where you live. Bigger towns and cities will have more websites devoted to them. This actually makes the job a little harder because there will be so much to choose from. Things to look out for include:

- The layout, design and navigation of the websites.
- What is their purpose, length and complexity?
- What special features do they have?
- How do you think the website is funded?
- How many mouse clicks does it take to find out what you need to know?
- Do they use plenty of graphics and images? If so, how are they used?
- Can you easily contact the site owner?

- Can visitors buy anything on the website?
- Can visitors book anything on the website?
- How do you know that the information is correct and unbiased?
- What is the overall look? Is it messy, jumbled and confused, or is there a consistent style?
- How easy is it to read the text and how large are the photographs?

Part Two

This task gives you an opportunity to really show that you know how to design a web page and that you understand what features need to be included to make it effective. Things to consider are:

- Will you use a logo?
- What colour scheme will you use?
- Will you use graphics and photographs?
- Is your text easy to read?
- Is your navigation as simple as possible?
- Will users need any special software to run any applications or features on your website?
- What will be on your home page and how often would you intend to update it?
- Can users communicate with you and do you encourage contributions from them?

Speak the language index